HAU
LIVERI

For Katie and Morgan Hague

© Tom Slemen 2003

Published by The Bluecoat Press, Liverpool
Book design by March Design, Liverpool
Front cover doll supplied by Rosie March
Printed by The Universities Press, Belfast

ISBN 1 904438 07 5

Tom Slemen

HAUNTED
LIVERPOOL 7

The Bluecoat Press

Contents

INTRODUCTION

What is a ghost? The first two relevant entries for 'ghost' in the *Oxford English Dictionary*, state: ¹Soul or spirit, as principle of life, as in 'give up the ghost'; Spirit of God, or Holy Ghost. ² Soul of a dead person appearing to the living; apparition, spectre. The same dictionary tells me that a soul is: 'the spiritual or immaterial part of man.'

In my opinion, these definitions of ghosts and the mysterious soul are inaccurate and misleading. To begin with, let us look at the first definition concerning a ghost being the soul of a person appearing to the living. There is a branch of philosophy called metaphysics, which is simply a Greek word which means 'that which comes after physics'. The Greek philosopher Aristotle left us a manuscript about his meditations on physics, and a series of papers containing his philosophical ramblings were also found with the manuscript. Because these papers were bunched together after the main work, or after the physics manuscript, they were termed Aristotle's Metaphysics – that which comes after physics. The word 'metaphysics' quickly entered the Greek lexicon as a label for a branch of philosophy dealing with such abstract concepts as time, space, being, substance and identity. I am not going to bore you with the various theories and hypotheses of the metaphysicians, but they did try, unsuccessfully, to solve what is known as the mind-body problem. In a nutshell, this problem can be basically summed up with the question: 'Where does the mind end and the body begin?'

Here's another way of looking at the problem without going into an Open University type of lecture. You are reading this book now, and the pages are inanimate, as dead as a Dodo (except perhaps that the paper might be crawling with various microscopic dust mites or bacteria). The hands that hold the book are alive, and contain amazing living cells with DNA that is millions of years old. The mind that is reading and considering these words is conscious and truly alive, so there is clearly a world of inanimate objects – a rock for example – and there is also the mental world of the mind.

In the world of our minds we can experience abstract thoughts and feelings such as pleasure, pain, jealousy and humour. We have consciousness – something that is very difficult to define. Some say consciousness is the soul, an invisible essence, or spark of life, given to us from God. Psychologists so far have been unable to explain what consciousness is, and many have been driven to a nervous breakdown trying to unravel the conundrum. There are down-to-earth psychologists and physicists who dismiss talk of a soul as utter claptrap. They believe consciousness is just an illusion, but they are still talking about something they can't fully explain, even though they are reluctant to admit their ignorance. I personally do believe in the soul, not out of some blind faith, or religious indoctrination, but simply because of the evidence I see around me. Nature is a ruthless mistress who only allows the strong to endure and multiply. The weak go to the wall. If a rat is born deformed, it is left to die. If a lion in the veldt is born blind, it will soon starve.

A scientist named Charles Darwin realised this basic law in the nineteenth century, and later rocked the establishment of the day by publishing *Origin of the Species* in 1859. In this landmark book, Darwin arrogantly dispensed with the necessity of a God, and claimed that today's species of plants and animals are descended from more primitive species that existed before them. Before Darwin, thinkers such as our old friend Aristotle had stated that species were eternally fixed and unchangeable. Darwin argued simply that this wasn't so – that all of the species living today had evolved from inferior versions of that species. This worried the Biblical fundamentalists – people who literally believe that everything the Bible states is fact; particularly believing that God created the world and all that lived upon it within six days.

Then came the bombshell. Charles Darwin declared that man himself was an animal, and an animal which was descended from a much more primitive version of a human being. What's more, his studies had convinced him that humans and apes shared a common ancestor, so in a way, the apes were our cousins!

It is easy to imagine the shockwaves of outrage which were generated by Darwin's theory. How could Adam and Eve, the first humans, possibly be cousins of the hairy beasts of the jungle? The trauma the Victorians felt would be comparable to your aunt turning up at your home with an orang utan and introducing him as some cousin you never knew you had.

Darwin introduced the concept of 'survival of the fittest' in his revolutionary theory. The animals that were physically weak, or unable to adapt to their environment, soon met with extinction, whereas the animals that adapted were able to survive and reproduce more of their successful kind. This would mean that man was merely a very successful animal who had adapted supremely well to his environment over millions of years, unlike his extinct 'relations' – the Cro Magnon and Neanderthal peoples.

Now, if Darwin's theory was true – and it does at first glance seem to make a lot of sense – then we humans are streamlined biological machines, honed to almost perfect efficiency, with no room for any excess baggage. The facts, however, soon point to many faults with Darwinian theory. Firstly, we have consciousness. Why on earth would we need that? If our only purpose on this planet was to survive and procreate, why would we need consciousness? Why on earth do we need literature, art and poetry? Why do we formulate laws that fly in the face of the great struggle for survival? Murder shouldn't be illegal, because killing rivals would be a good way to ensure our own survival, yet we have ethical laws that universally state that killing is wrong, and even capital punishment for convicted murderers has been outlawed in many parts of the world.

Inside our globular head, beneath a dangerously thin skull, we have a brain that is oversized and out of all proportion to our everyday needs. Why this brain is so over-endowed is one of the strange facts that chips away at the edifice of Charles Darwin's theory of evolution. Our brain is one forty-fifth of our body weight, and the gorilla's brain is one two-hundredth of its body weight. There is clearly an enormous gulf between the apes and man. They are content to live in the jungle, whilst we are restlessly in search of other worlds and are forever amassing new knowledge. The birds may use the stars to navigate, but we are the only animals who wonder about them when we look at the night sky.

Alfred Russell Wallace, a great friend of Charles Darwin, came to the very same conclusion as me. He reluctantly decided that the law of evolution did not apply to the species of Homo Sapiens – man. Wallace wrote to Darwin about his grave doubts: 'Nature never over-endows a species beyond the demands of everyday existence.' Darwin wrote a garbled, emotional reply about Wallace destroying his theory, which he described as the murder of his 'child', and beneath the letter he had written the word 'No!' underlined three times.

Wallace's observation about the massive cubic capacity of the human brain, its superfluous talents and, in terms of survival, frivolous interests in art, music and literature, is as relevant today as it was in the nineteenth century, and remains unexplained.

This leads me back to the original question, what is a ghost? I don't think a ghost is the manifestation of the soul of a deceased person, as the *Oxford Dictionary* states. The soul, as the metaphysicians have established, is quite a separate thing from the body, just as a motorist bears no physical resemblance to the vehicle he drives. The soul is the driver and the body is the vehicle. The soul is not a ghost. Some ghosts aren't even alive and possess no consciousness.

A case in point is the soulless apparition of the 'Ghost Bus of Kensington'.

Throughout the 1930s, dozens of motorists and pedestrians reported seeing a red double-decker London bus bearing the Number 7 route number in the North Kensington area of the capital. Long after dark, when all bus services had ceased to run, the red Number 7 bus would appear out of nowhere, usually at the junction of St Mark's Road and Cambridge Gardens – a point which had something of a reputation as being a dangerous corner. The bus would tear along the road with no one in the driving seat and not a single passenger onboard. Many motorists swerving to avoid the phantom bus would crash, and several died as a result.

One report to the Kensington police sums up the bizarre haunting: 'I was turning the corner and saw a bus tearing towards me. The lights of the top and bottom decks and the headlights were full on, but I could see no sign of crew or passengers. I yanked my steering wheel hard over, and mounted the pavement, scraping the roadside wall. The bus just vanished.'

Another report was given a lot of credence because it was made by a local transport official who had been startled to see the ghost bus drive itself into the bus depot in the early hours of the morning. The bus came to a halt, and its engine could be heard purring away. Seconds later, the entire bus vanished into thin air.

Why a bus should haunt the roads of Kensington remains a mystery, but some thought it was significant that the hauntings stopped as soon as the dangerous corner where it appeared was altered in the interests of public safety.

The phantom bus of Kensington is not a unique case. There are other ghostly vehicles that roam the roads after dark, including an old single-decker bus that runs along Liverpool's Grove Street now and then. I mentioned the ectoplasmic vehicle in the first volume of *Haunted Liverpool*.

It's clear from these cases that some ghosts do not require souls, and were never alive to begin with. In my own researches over the years, I have classified basically six types of ghost. These are:

1 **Carnate** A carnate is a solid-looking entity which you can touch, and it can interact with witnesses. Carnates may be responsible for some 'phantom hitch-hiker' incidents, where the ghost seems tangible.

Here is an alleged photograph of a discarnate ghost named Myra, a University of Missouri student who departed this life in 1869. She initially contacted members of SORRAT (Society for Research on Rapport and Telekinesis) through a rap code, and subsequently appeared before them and several other witnesses on 27 June 1967, to allow the psychical researchers to take her photograph.

This second photograph depicts what is alleged to be 'McKenzie's ghost' – a solid looking phantom who haunts Rodney Street, close to the cemetery where his mortal remains are enclosed in a pyramidal tomb. See Volumes One and Four of *Haunted Liverpool* for the tale behind McKenzie's spectre.

2 **Discarnate** A discarnate is an entity that has no physical body. Discarnates usually manifest themselves after a drop in temperature (perhaps as they absorb thermal energy from the environment to 'power-up'). Poltergeists are usually discarnate. Some discarnate beings are spirits that have never lived in a body.

Here is a photograph of damage done to the bed of John Glynn (pictured), in 1952, by a powerful poltergeist at Runcorn. The case is mentioned in *Haunted Liverpool*, volume one.

The picture below shows an artist's impression of the so-called Runcorn poltergeist when it chose to manifest itself.

3 **Psychological** These 'ghosts' Are hallucinations which appear to one person for various subjective reasons: Hypnagogic (border of sleep) visions, tricks of the light (optical illusions), drugs, drink, schizophrenia, etc.

Here is an example of an optical illusion that tricks the brain into seeing either an old hag or a young lady.

4 **Doppelgangers** Doppelgangers are 'phantasms of the living'; projected images of a living person who is ill or experiencing a crisis. Some doppelgangers may not actually be a ghostly twin at all, but people who were teleported from one place to another by a phenomenon that is also known as bi-location. In the 1970s, three teenaged girls walking along Dunnings Bridge Road suddenly found themselves walking near Aintree Racecourse a mile away – a classic case of teleportation.

6 **Re-enacting ghosts** Solid or semi-transparent images and sounds of people and inanimate objects which appear to be limited in their movements and merely re-enact a specific scene at periodic intervals. These ghosts seem to be little more than hologram recordings from the past. Or could someone or something else in the future be 'replaying' historical events by tinkering with time?

Here is an example of a re-enacting ghost (pictured), a ghostly horse-drawn carriage that has been seen hurtling down Bibby Lane in Bootle, and has even rushed straight through several unfortunate pedestrians who suffered no physical harm, but sustained psychological trauma!

A classic example of a re-enactment ghost is the phantom housemaid who walks up a particular flight of stairs, at a particular house in Aigburth, since the 1870s. The ghost has not been seen to do anything else.

7 **Extra-dimensional beings** These are entities which originate from outside our dimension and possibly even our space-time continuum. An example that comes to mind is of the strange, spindly, grey-coloured beings that allegedly appeared when occultists tried to conjure up the Devil in a ward in the derelict John Bagot hospital in northern Liverpool in the 1970s. The figures bore an uncanny resemblance to the so-called 'Greys' who feature in many modern UFO abduction cases. The beings that appeared in John Bagot hospital said they were only separated from our world by a wafer-thin dimension that allowed them to observe us at very close quarters. They also said that they could sometimes reach through the thin dimensional partition to snatch people. Other information imparted by the entities was so terrifying, that the Satanists fled from the disused hospital, and several of them died shortly after the unearthly encounter.

In this picture a journalist examines the encircled eight-pointed star which Satanists had drawn on the floor of the derelict ward in the closed down John Bagot Hospital in the 1970s.

~

That is my taxonomy of ghosts. If you should meet a ghost, remember that the person who stays put, sees more than the person who turns and runs! Try and stay calm, cool and collected. Furthermore, if there are still sceptics reading this far into the book who would scoff at the idea of ghosts, consider that you may be a spectre yourself one day.

THE ART OF BLACKMAIL

On the night of Saturday 3 January 1863, the Lord Mayor of Liverpool held a magnificent party at the Concert Hall in Lord Nelson Street. Over two thousand guests, drawn from the high society of the North West, attended the lavish soirée, and all proceeds were to go to a charity for the poor of the area.

Among the illustrious guests was a very mysterious man who introduced himself as Benjamin Julius, a fine artist who had been commissioned on many occasions to paint portraits of the highest people in the land. Mr Julius was also an exceptionally good raconteur – capturing audiences wherever he went with his sparkling anecdotes and ready wit. He would thrill his listeners with tales of the Prince of Wales, with whom he was acquainted, and he could not resist mentioning that he had received an invitation to the Prince's forthcoming marriage to Princess Alexandra of Denmark.

Later in the evening Mr Julius flamboyantly struck a Lucifer match, let it burn awhile, then blew it out and used its charred end to swiftly execute a flattering charcoal sketch of one of the female guests on a napkin. Lady Leonora Cunningham was captivated by the artist to such an extent that she subsequently commissioned him to paint a portrait of her at his attic studio on Falkner Street. With due deference and ceremony, Leonora was ushered up to the artist's studio and Julius positioned his illustrious subject before the diffuse morning sunlight filtering through the northern window. The artist worked in a fevered frenzy, with a tortured look of utmost determination to fix the vision of feminine beauty before him to mere canvas.

Incredibly, within a span of eight hours, having barely stopped to take a break, the full-length oil portrait was finished. However, when the exhausted Lady Leonora inspected it, the colour drained from her face, and she had to sit down and compose herself. In the painting, instead of the pose she had been meticulously holding all day, she was confronted by a picture of herself inexplicably cradling a baby boy with red curly hair in her arms.

"What on earth is, is – that?" Lady Leonora gasped, tears welling in her eyes.

"Why, it's young Archie, don't you recognise him? That young son of yours that you're hiding from the world," Mr Julius replied, sombrely, his face betraying no emotion.

Leonora Cunningham certainly did recognise the red-haired child, he was the celebrated lady's darkest secret, the result of an ill-advised affair with the dashing, red-headed Captain Lunt, two years before.

Lady Leonora had tried for seven long years to conceive a child by her husband, but had produced no offspring. So when Lord Cunningham discovered that she was pregnant, his suspicions were immediately aroused. Uncovering the affair after some investigation, and realising that his wife was carrying another man's child, he ordered her to rid herself of it, but she desperately wanted to keep the child and refused to take such a painful course of action. To try and avert a scandal as the pregnancy advanced, Lord Cunningham announced that his wife had recently been taken ill, and was now recuperating in North Wales. When her Ladyship returned, accompanied by the baby with the telltale red hair, her husband immediately had the infant placed in an orphanage, away from public inspection, angrily declaring to his wife that the baby was not of his own flesh and blood, and he could therefore never have any affection for it.

Lady Leonora was desperate to know how Mr Julius had found out about her closely guarded secret, and she warned him to destroy the portrait at once, or face legal action. Instead of being chastened by the wrath of such an elevated personage, his response was simply to tell her to: "Take it to the courts, Madam! I will drag the sordid secrets of you and your husband out into the open for every newspaper in the country to print!"

Lady Leonora therefore had no choice but to purchase the painting for £4000, and she later had it destroyed.

There were many more victims of the diabolically devious Mr Julius, including a wealthy businessman named George Heap, the proprietor of several Lancashire rice mills.

In the August of 1863, Mr Julius cordially welcomed Mr Heap into his studio and asked him to adopt the naturalistic pose of lighting a pipe, as the mill-owner was a pipe-smoker. The artist then proceeded to paint Heap's portrait, but when it was finished, his subject gazed at the finished result in absolute horror. In the painting, George Heap had indeed been depicted holding a lighted match, apparently to light his pipe, but through a window behind him could be seen a very familiar building ablaze – the rice mill which Heap owned in Pownall Square.

Only a few weeks before, that mill had been completely gutted by a mysterious fire, and Heap had received a mammoth insurance payment as a result. To any local person looking at the painting, it would immediately suggest that Heap was responsible for setting fire to his own factory, obviously for financial gain.

In fact, most merchants in Liverpool already suspected that this had been the case. Realising that he had been duped, and incandescent with rage, Heap refused to pay for the scandalous painting, and insisted that it be destroyed at once. Mr Julius was completely unabashed, as usual, declaring that he had no intention of destroying such a wonderful piece of art, and that if Mr Heap refused to pay for it, he would have to exhibit it privately, to recoup his losses. On hearing this, Heap panicked and realised that he had no choice but to pay an undisclosed sum for the artistic work of blackmail.

An entry in the diary of Lady Leonora Cunningham states that, in 1865, the sinister Benjamin Julius thankfully suddenly vanished without trace from the Liverpool scene, leaving his Falkner Street studio deserted. Perhaps he had reached a point where it was impossible for him to dupe any more people in the city without being exposed as a blackmailer, and had gone off to look for more fertile pastures elsewhere. No doubt Lady Leonora was heartily relieved to at last be rid of her artistic tormentor. As for George Heap, he later remarked of the portraitist, "I am sure that he is the Devil in disguise".

CATCH THE BALL

The ancient megalithic Calder Stones of Calderstones Park, in Liverpool, feature strange carvings of occult symbols and engraved maps of star constellations and spiral galaxies. The stones are thought to belong to the late Neolithic period, but no one is absolutely sure, and the entire area now occupied by the park in which the stones stand, has long been regarded as a mystical site. Could the mysterious background of the park have some bearing on the following tale, which I have pieced together over the years from the memories of some of the older denizens of Wavertree and Woolton?

Around 1953, three thirteen-year-old Liverpool schoolboys – Kenny, Johnny and Bobby – rendezvoused in Calderstones Park one morning to play cricket in the summer sunshine. Kenny brought along a cricket bat, Johnny produced an old scuffed tennis ball and Bobby's rolled-up jumper would serve as the wicket. During play, Kenny bowled and Johnny hit the ball for six – towards a gnarled, thousand-year-old tree called the Allerton Oak, whose branches had spread so wide that their enormous weight had to be supported by iron props, like crutches. The ball was fielded by an old white-bearded vagrant who was sitting on a bench close to the old tree. The boys yelled at him to throw the ball back, but the old man just sat there, staring into the park, seemingly oblivious to their cries. The three teenagers ran over and Johnny said, "Give us our ball back!"

Instead of handing over the ball, the man just smiled, and patted the bench besides him.

"Sit down a minute, lads. I have a few tales to tell you," he said.

The boys noticed that the old man's rheumy eyes were covered with a pale blue film, as if he had a cataract problem. But there was something strangely compelling about him, and the three boys sat down next to him and listened as he told them many strange and fabulous tales which kept them completely enthralled. Halfway through the storytelling, the old man pointed to the boating lake and said, "The Devil's Swan rides on the water there now and then, and if you see him, someone will die in your family."

The three boys shuddered and glanced nervously at the ducks and geese on the lake and then at each other. The man then said something which really excited the three boys.

"Did you know that one of you three will be the most famous man in the world one day?" he asked.

Naturally, the first thing the boys wanted to know was which of them he was talking about, and by way of reply, the silvery-haired storyteller held up the grubby, old tennis ball and held it before them.

"This will decide!" he said.

"I'd watch him if I were you, he's potty," a park warden advised the boys, as he saw them eagerly following after the old man, who was still holding the tennis ball out in front of him, as if it were some kind of divining rod.

With everything they had ever been told about not talking to strangers going right out of their heads, the they followed the old vagrant, who, like a latter day pied piper, led them right out of the park, across several roads, to a bridge nearly a mile away, overlooking a railway track on Rose Lane, Mossley Hill.

"Now boys," he said, "listen very carefully. When the train comes, I will throw this ball down the funnel, and the steam will shoot it right up into the air by the time it emerges from the other side of this bridge. The boy who catches the ball will be the most famous man in the world one day."

To an adult, such an outlandish prediction would have seemed utterly preposterous, but to Bobby, Kenny and Johnny, it was a magical challenge,

19

and one which they were very keen to rise to. Presently, the train came thundering down the track, puffing a white plume of steam out of its funnel. The man leaned right over the bridge so that the guard-rail was pressed to his navel, with his left arm holding the tennis ball aloft. As the engine arrived below him, he was engulfed in a dense cloud of smoke and steam, and through all the hissing and chugging, the boys could hear him cry, "Bull's eye!"

The locomotive rattled the bridge beneath their feet and the three excited boys watched the steam erupt from the other side. Just as the old man had predicted, the tennis ball shot skywards from the cloud, then slowed and came falling back to earth, propelled on a curved trajectory by a sudden gust of wind. Being the most competitive, Kenny pushed his friends to the ground in the scramble to catch the ball, and focused hard as he tried to gauge where it would land. But the ball slipped through his hands – and Johnny just managed to catch it before it hit the ground. Johnny jumped up from the pavement, waving the scruffy tennis ball in triumph. He turned to show it to the old man, but he had inexplicably vanished into thin air. They searched the area around the bridge, but he was nowhere to be found.

"The whole thing's stupid anyway," Bobby told Johnny. "He was having us on – how could you be the most famous man in the world? You should be so lucky, you skinny little whipper snapper!"

"Yeah! He was just a daft old man, like that parkie said," agreed a sour-faced Kenny. "All that Devil's swan rubbish!"

"Well I won, anyway," said Johnny, philosophically.

"Race you back to the park," said Bobby. "Last one there's a sissy!"

And Bobby Smith, Kenny Greene and Johnny Lennon ran away from the bridge and back to the park and their game of cricket.

A PLACE TO PLAY

The following story was related to me many years ago by an old blind woman in Wavertree. Her name was Molly, and the tale she told to me begins on a snowy Victorian winter afternoon.

On Sunday 23 December 1894, a poverty-stricken nine-year-old girl with the quaint name of Rosie Sparks, left her crumbling home on Cow Lane – which is now Prince Alfred Road – and went out to play in the snow with

Chip, her little mongrel dog. To Rosie's delight, a deep ivory blanket of snow had completely covered the cobbles on Cow Lane, transforming her normally dismal playground, into a winter wonderland. She began to make a snowman, beginning by rolling a ball of snow round and round until it was the size of a barrel. She was so completely taken up with the task, that she was oblivious to the biting cold as she stood on the snowy cobbles in her bare feet and patted the snow with her thin, mittenless hands.

In the distance there was a huge old mansion called the Grange, set in about one hundred acres of private land. It was a spooky looking house, surrounded by old twisted trees, whose bare skeletons rattled and scraped at the windows on this cold December day, blown by the chill winter winds. An elderly, crooked man called Walter Tregeagle roamed the grounds, carrying an old sword and a blunderbuss. He was a type of gamekeeper cum watchman, and was very brutal to any trespassers found on the land, be they men, women or children.

The Grange had once been the residence of wealthy merchant Samuel Graves, up until his death in 1873. But now the Grange estate was home to a very strange and sinister man. No one knew his name, and very few ever caught so much as a glimpse of him. Many wild rumours were circulating about the mysterious resident of the mansion – some claimed he was a rich recluse who had shunned the world after being jilted by his fiancée. Others said he was no longer able to live among humanity because he was severely disfigured. Gossip was rife, but nobody really knew anything definite.

But upon this wintry afternoon, Rosie Sparks was destined to find out the truth about the identity of the enigmatic newcomer.

Rosie was so engrossed in building her snowman that she didn't notice that Chip had gone missing until she had finished it. She went home and looked for him, but he wasn't there. She looked everywhere. Then a lad named Topper Murphy – so called because he wore a battered old top hat – said he had seen Chip chase a cat through the railings of the entrance gate to the Grange. Rosie and Topper ran up to the gate, and the little girl shouted for her dog, but he didn't turn up. The house and gardens looked so beautiful in the snow that Rosie bravely decided that she would risk climbing over the gate. Topper helped her, but he was too afraid of old Mr Tregeagle to follow her.

"I'll wait here, Rosie," he told her, and waited anxiously at the gate, expecting to see Mr Tregeagle at any moment.

Rosie was cautiously threading her way through the trees and snow-covered hedges, when a large heavy snow cloud drifted over the estate, darkening the skies and bringing with it an oppressive gloom. Rosie shivered as the pretty scene was transformed into something altogether more sinister. She crouched lower and kept her eyes peeled for Chip, not even daring to whisper his name now that she was inside the gates – then she froze as she felt something sharp and ice-cold brush the nape of her neck.

Paralysed with foreboding, she heard a bronchial cackle of laughter behind her, and slowly turned to see the dreaded gamekeeper, Walter Tregeagle. He held a long sword which he pointed menacingly at the terrified girl, and was dressed in a faded and tatty scarlet British Army tunic. On his head he wore a ridiculously tall black military hat called a shako.

Tregeagle was a veteran of the Crimean War of 1855. Almost forty years had passed since the hostilities had ceased, but Tregeagle's mind had never recovered from the horrors of war. With twisted lips he snarled at poor Rosie.

"You're for it now, young miss," he said and placed the blade of the sword against the centre parting of her hair. "I'm going to slice you right down the middle!" And with a wicked smile, he lifted the sword, ready to strike.

Overcome with terror, and frozen to the marrow, the child passed out. She landed face down in the snow, and as she fell, Chip came bounding out of nowhere and started to snap at the gamekeeper's boots. Tregeagle swung the sword about furiously, missing the mongrel dog by inches. With his floppy ears pressed flat against his head in fear, Chip stood his ground between the demented old soldier and his mistress. But just then, in the nick of time, there came the sounds of feet crunching in the snow, and a well spoken voice floated in the air from nearby, "Mr Tregeagle! Mr Tregeagle! Stop that at once! Leave the poor child alone!"

The effect of the voice was immediate and electric – Tregeagle dropped the sword, straightened himself up and saluted. The man who had brought about this astonishing effect was wearing a bowler hat and a long black coat, and had a thick, woolly scarf wrapped around his face, so that only his eyes could be seen. He ordered Tregeagle to carry Rosie Sparks up to the mansion, where she was given a glass of warm milk laced with rum.

When Rosie revived, she recoiled in horror, because the man standing over her had no nose! Seeing her reaction, he covered his face below his eyes with a handkerchief, and gently asked her why she had been trespassing on his estate. Rosie explained that she had been looking for her dog, upon which Tregeagle, who had been watching his master's treatment of the girl with rising anger and frustration, suggested shooting the animal, but the man with the disfigured face dismissed the eccentric gamekeeper's suggestion with a wave of the hand.

The gentleman got into conversation with Rosie, and asked her about her life, what her home was like, and what she usually had to eat. He looked with pity at her ragged clothes and her chillblained feet. He seemed shocked and saddened when he heard about Rosie's life of poverty. The depressing streets and alleyways were her playground, and watery gruel her staple diet. Rosie liked the funny gentleman and innocently asked why he had no nose, to which he replied that he had been born that way.

He told Rosie about a girl he had once loved, and how he had been unable to approach her because of his deformed face. He cried unashamedly as he unburdened himself to her. At the end of his story he paced about in front of the fire, wiping the bitter tears from his eyes, then left the room and made his way to the pantry. He returned with a huge bone, covered with bits of meat. He gave it to Chip, but the dog had never seen a bone like it before, and wore himself out trying to tackle it.

Gazing thoughtfully into the blazing log fire, the man suddenly said, "Rosie, I will give you somewhere to play."

Later in the evening he gave Rosie a small green canvas bag full of guineas, then ordered Mr Tregeagle to escort her safely back to her house. In the bag of money there was a brief, sad note written by the mysterious gentleman. In the note, he disclosed that he was dying of a wasting disease, and wasn't expected to see the New Year. This proved to be true.

On Christmas Day, a funeral hearse was seen trundling into the estate, pulled by a team of gleaming black horses, with large ostrich-feather plumes tossing on their heads. In the May of the following year, the Grange and its adjoining properties were demolished, and the estate was levelled and grassed over, leaving no trace of the old mansion. A park was built on the land – a park which was named Wavertree Playground. Liverpool City Council was presented with this park by a deceased man in his will, with the stipulation that he was to remain anonymous. This man gave specific instructions in the document: 'The park is to be a place for the poor children to run and play in.'

Twelve thousand children were invited to the opening ceremony, and each of them was given free milk and cakes. The exciting day culminated in a grand fireworks display. One of the twelve thousand children was Rosie Sparks, and while all the other children were dashing about enjoying the novelty of the wide open spaces, she thought about the man with the unacceptable face, and she quietly whispered to herself a grateful, "Thank you".

Today, in Liverpool, children still play in the park that was donated to them by the mysterious, sad man from the Grange. Because the magnanimous gentleman's identity has never been discovered, the local residents aptly called the park 'The Mystery'.

Rosie Sparks grew up and had children of her own, and one of them was Molly, the woman who related the tale to me.

THE CAVEMAN OF VICTORIA PARK

This is one of the strangest, yet most touching, stories I have ever researched.

In 1870, in the Liverpool district of Wavertree, Patrick O'Connor, an iron-monger, lived with his wife at a house on North Drive, Victoria Park. The couple decided to adopt a baby girl who had been born blind, and they called her Jessica. Her own mother had died in childbirth, and the father, believe it or not, had callously abandoned the baby because she was blind. The sight of the helpless infant in the orphanage had tugged at Mrs O'Connor's heartstrings.

"When I saw Jessica lying there," she recalled, "unable to see and so helpless, I just knew I had to have her."

The strange story unfolded when Jessica was six, in 1876. Mrs O'Connor had now borne her husband a baby boy named William, and Jessica's life revolved around her cute little baby brother. Despite her disability, she was allowed to push his huge hooded pram around the back garden of the house on North Drive. Mrs O'Connor used to supervise Jessica most of the time, but not on one particular afternoon, when something terrible happened. Two boys climbed on top of the garden wall and one of them shouted, "Hah! Look! There's the stupid blind girl."

The other boy sneered and said: "She talks to herself as well, she must be mad."

The two boys started laughing and wolf-whistling. One of them threw a clod of dry earth, and it hit Jessica's forehead. The girl ran towards the house, crying hysterically, with tears and mud mingling on her face. The insensitive boys scarpered. Mrs O'Connor found her little daughter curled up under the kitchen table, distressed and sobbing.

That night, Mr O'Connor sat Jessica on his knee before bedtime.

"Are you going to say your prayers, Jess?" he asked.

The girl nodded, and said: "I have to thank Jesus for lots of things."

Mr O'Connor, knowing about the incident with the two boys, hugged her and said, "Really, pet?"

He took the child to her bedroom and watched her kneel at the bottom of her bed. Jessica earnestly recited the Lord's Prayer, then added her own, more personal prayers: "Thank you, Lord, for the sun that I love feeling on my face, and when the dragonflies hum. Thank you for the nice smells of the flowers in the garden. And thank you for the sound of my baby brother when he laughs. I love him and have told him about you."

Tears rolled down Mr O'Connor's face – he felt so humbled by this child who never complained about her disability, and was so thankful for all the things that most people don't even have time to notice. Then he heard her whisper something which intrigued him. "Thank you for my secret friend," she added, and smiled from ear to ear.

Mr O'Connor told his wife about Jessica's reference to her mysterious friend, and was surprised to find that she already knew.

"She's told me all about him. He's a caveman. Well, from her descriptions he is. She says he's a huge man with long hair, and that he wears animal furs. He carries a big axe too."

"She must have overheard someone talking about cavemen. She's got a good imagination, God bless her."

Autumn arrived, and Mr O'Connor collected all the fallen leaves and burnt them at the end of the garden. That night, his wife was in the kitchen, when she happened to look out of the window. She saw the smouldering embers of the burning pile of leaves – then she noticed the shadow of a strange-looking man crouched down by the fire. His unkempt hair was very long, and he had a straggly beard which reached nearly down to his navel. His arms were grubby and bare, and so was his chest.

Mrs O'Connor ran up the four flights of stairs to wake her husband, who'd decided to have an early night. The alerted and alarmed Patrick O'Connor ran downstairs with a shotgun, and peeped out of the kitchen window, but could see nothing but the smouldering leaves. Mrs O'Connor insisted that she had seen a strange man at the fire, and she gave a full description, but her husband just shrugged his shoulders, bolted the door, and went back to bed, yawning and shaking his head.

A few days later, Jessica came into the house wearing a strange, primitive bracelet. It was made from small pieces of sharp stone of different colours. Mr O'Connor recognised some of the stones as flints. When they asked who had given her the bracelet, she looked very sheepish, and eventually said that the caveman had. This made the O'Connor family feel decidedly uneasy. Who was this strange friend of hers? Was he a figment of her imagination? Or did he really exist? After all, Mrs O'Connor had said that she had seen someone in the garden, who, to all intents and purposes, looked like a caveman – and she wasn't given to flights of fancy.

Shortly afterwards, an elderly neighbour reported seeing the ghostly caveman in broad daylight, wandering about the O'Connors' garden. She claimed that he was wearing animal furs and had leathery strips of animal skin wrapped around his legs and feet. He also carried what seemed to be a crude axe. One moment he was there, the next he was gone.

Mr O'Connor was finally convinced when he heard a commotion on North Drive. The two boys who had tormented Jessica came running into the O'Connors' shop on the High Street, saying that a mad tramp had attacked them, and that he was in Mr O'Connor's garden. Patrick O'Connor went to investigate, and there, at the end of the garden, was the fabled caveman, stooping down over Jessica with a smile on his face.

"What's your game?" O'Connor shouted, and the ghost backed away as the ironmonger approached. The phantom backed away until it vanished into the garden wall.

Mr O'Connor grabbed the child and ran into the house with her. From that day he was a convert, who admitted that there were such things as ghosts. He told a friend who had built the house which was then occupied by the O'Connors about the ghost, and the builder told him that in 1867, during the construction of the houses on North Drive, workmen uncovered a number of Bronze Age burial urns, dating from before 1000 BC, containing human remains and flint arrowheads.

Worried about his daughter's safety, Mr O'Connor begged the local priest to bless the garden, and the apparition of the caveman was seen no more.

Also, on a happy note, three years later, little Jessica was struck down with whooping cough. She survived, and as a side effect, she regained her sight. The first thing she saw was her little brother's smiling face.

India Rubber Menace

In 1949, a cargo of India rubber arrived at Liverpool Docks. In the hold of the same cargo ship, there were several crates of African artifacts, including shrunken heads, tribal spears and shields, and several elaborately carved wooden masks, which were used by the witchdoctors of a Nigerian tribe. These items were destined to be exhibited at the Liverpool Museum in William Brown Street.

During the unloading of the African artifacts, a crate slipped from the winch cables, and it crashed down on to the quayside, spilling its exotic contents. The dockers and stevedores quickly collected as many items as they could stuff into their pockets. One particular light-fingered docker named Georgie, decided to keep one of the wooden masks, as he thought it would make a nice talking point on his parlour wall. Two other dockers each pilfered a shrunken head. They thought no one would notice the absence of a couple of the heads, as there had been about twenty of them in the crate.

However, all three dockers suffered amazing bad luck later that day. During the lunch break, one of the dockers, a man named Brian, was playing a game of poker in a hut on the waterfront, and was winning every game until he had amassed about fifty pounds, which was a very substantial sum of money in 1949. When the lunchbreak ended, the dockers left the hut, and just as Brian was gloating over winning such a large amount of money, a sudden gale force gust of wind came out of nowhere and battered the quayside. The wind slammed open the door of the hut, sending ten shilling notes fluttering out across the waterfront like confetti. Dockers scrambled to grab the notes, but every last one of them blew into the River Mersey. Next thing, the mysterious wind died down and it became calm again. Furious at having watched his winnings disappear before his eyes, Brian took the shrunken head out of his jacket and wondered if it could possibly be cursed.

About an hour later, Alan, the other docker who had taken one of the shrunken heads, also experienced a terrible bit of bad luck. Alan wore an eyepatch because he had lost his eye during the war when a piece of shrapnel from a bomb exploding at the docks damaged his right eyeball beyond repair. Alan walked into a warehouse where two young sons of one of the dockers were playing darts. The dartboard was mounted on a door. Alan opened that door just as one of the men threw a dart – and it shot straight through the pupil of Alan's good eye. He collapsed from traumatic shock. Luckily, he was later treated by a highly skilled Rodney Street surgeon, and his remaining eye was saved, but it was never the same again after that freak accident.

That same day, in the late afternoon, a large pallet, measuring about twenty-five feet square, was loaded with several huge, trussed-up blocks of India rubber, and the crane operator was expertly transporting the rubber cargo from the ship on to the quayside – when, for reasons that have never been properly explained, the four chains linked to the pallet snapped simultaneously. The huge block of India rubber plummeted sixty feet, and the dockers below yelled out to one another and fanned out from the pallet, like ripples on a lake. Everyone scattered – everyone except one docker named Georgie, the one who had stolen the African mask. He looked up in total horror as the block of rubber raced directly towards him. Georgie ran as fast as his legs could carry him, and just managed to get clear in time. The huge bulk of the bale of rubber smashed into the quayside – and then it bounced back into the air.

Now, India rubber is very elastic. Some of the older readers may remember a thing called the 'superball' which was sold in shops in the 1970s. The superball was a small ball of India rubber, which, when hurled down at the ground, would rebound as high as a house and continue bouncing for quite some time.

So Georgie ran down the quayside with the bale of India rubber bouncing crazily after him, almost as if it had a mind of its own, and was in deliberate pursuit. Wherever the terrified docker ran, the gigantic block of rubber followed. Georgie ran across a road, and the rubber went that way too, bouncing twenty-five feet into the air after him. It landed on a horse-drawn cart at one point, completely flattening the vehicle and injuring the unfortunate horse into the bargain. Georgie ran back across the road, and the bouncing block followed him. In the end, the exhausted and terrified docker dived into the Huskisson Branch Dock to get away from the bouncing bale – and it bounced straight in after him! Georgie tried to resurface but the rubber bale was blocking his way and he had to swim out from under it, which was no easy feat.

He was later treated at the Northern Hospital for shock. He soon told his friends to take the African mask from his locker and to take it personally to Liverpool Museum. Georgie said that when he was being pursued by the block of Indian rubber, he had distinctly heard weird laughter. He was convinced that some sort of malevolent African spirit had been deliberately guiding the bouncing rubber block towards him!

FRANCESCA

On the foggy Sunday evening of 18 December 1904, forty-five-year-old Mary Eccles of Mill Lane rushed into the Police Station on Wavertree High Street and told the station sergeant James Anderson, that her eleven-year-old daughter Lucy had gone missing again.

"Not again! You shouldn't let her out of your sight, Mrs Eccles. You know what she's like," Mr Anderson moaned.

His superior, Inspector John Crompton, told the sergeant to go and look in all the usual places for the wayward young girl. With a disgruntled sigh, Sergeant Anderson gulped down his mug of cocoa, donned his helmet and cape, and set out into the cold fog to search for Lucy Eccles, or the 'Wild Child of Wavertree' as she was known.

Ever since Lucy's father had passed away two years before, the girl's behaviour had become steadily worse. Just a few days ago she had gone missing, and had been found by a search party in the highest reaches of a tree in the grounds of Sandown Hall. On a previous occasion, during the summer, outraged anglers had reported the girl to the police after she decided to divest herself of all her clothes and go for a swim in Wavertree Fish Pond!

On this fog-enshrouded December night, the grumbling Sergeant Anderson searched orchards, parks, a deserted cottage on Olive Lane, and many of the usual haunts of the uncontrollable girl, but Lucy was nowhere to be found. Just when the policeman was about to give up the search, he saw Lucy emerging from the jade green fog in Wavertree Nook Road, carrying a small, under-nourished mongrel dog.

"Mr Anderson, I found a dog, look!" the girl told him, excitedly.

Sergeant Anderson shook his head – she seemed to have no understanding of the trouble she caused her family and the police. He scolded her for wandering off, knowing full well that anything he said would go in one ear and out the other, and returned her to her mother on Mill Lane. Knowing that Lucy would throw a terrible tantrum if she tried to make her abandon the dog, Mrs Eccles reluctantly allowed her to keep the scruffy little animal. Lucy named the dog Luke. Her gallivanting continued, and Luke would follow her for miles around Liverpool, getting into all kinds of mischief with his new friend.

One summer evening in 1905, Lucy and Luke were exploring the neighbourhood of Fairfield, when Lucy found a jointed porcelain doll among a pile of refuse in the courtyard of a house. Lucy took an instant liking to the doll, but Luke seemed to regard the toy with great suspicion. When Mrs Eccles saw the doll, she asked Lucy if she had given her a name, and her daughter shrugged and said, "Just Dolly I suppose, Ma."

That evening there was a loud yelp upstairs. Luke came bounding downstairs and dived under a chair, cowering with fear. Lucy came down from her room and exclaimed, "Ma! That doll's alive! It said it's name's Francesca, and she dances too!"

Mrs Eccles just smiled, she was used to her daughter's tall tales and usually ignored them. Without looking up, she concentrated on darning the stocking she was holding. Lucy jumped up and down in frustration, and angrily yelled: "It's alive, Ma. It's alive!"

Lucy took her mother by the hand and dragged her up the stairs, but when they went into the bedroom, 'Francesca' was lying limp and lifeless on the bed. Lucy grabbed the doll and shook it, shouting, "Speak! Please speak again!" But the doll remained silent and motionless. Lucy insisted that the doll could speak and dance, and her mother sighed, "I believe you, dear," then left the room wondering why her daughter was so difficult.

That night, Mrs Eccles heard Lucy singing in her bedroom, and another voice was singing along with her. The words of the song were, "Alouette, gentille Alouette, Alouette je te plumerai." More than a little surprised, Mrs Eccles left her bed and stood outside the door of her daughter's room, listening to the two singing voices. She bent down and peeped through the keyhole. Francesca the doll was dancing up and down on the end of the bed! Mrs Eccles recoiled in shock, then shouted Lucy and barged into the room. Instantly the doll fell down off the bed and lay motionless on the floor.

On the following day, while Lucy was at school, Mrs Eccles visited a priest and told him about the dancing doll. He came to the house, and when he saw the doll, he recognised it at once. It had belonged to a child of well-to-do parents in Fairfield who had lost their ten-year-old daughter, Lily, after she had succumbed to a long illness. Her doll had indeed been called Francesca, and her favourite song had been *Alouette*. Mrs Eccles became uneasy when she heard this, but the priest advised her to keep the apparently haunted doll and assured her that Lily had been a beautiful and good child, and the doll might be a good influence on Lucy. The doll was returned to Lucy's room, and strangely enough, her unruly behaviour gradually lessened, she settled down and even began to excel at school.

MONKEY SNATCH

On the beautiful sunny Saturday of 9 July 1870, a Mr William Judcote, a seventy-year-old property tycoon from Liverpool, sat in his high-backed wicker chair admiring the colourful flowery acres of his garden. Behind him stood his white cottage with its picture postcard thatched roof, a country retreat situated in Manxbridge, a small cosy village in Somerset. Mr Judcote sipped a measure of fine whiskey, and watched his exotic pet, Hulch, climbing a sycamore tree. Hulch was a powerful, muscular monkey who measured over five feet in height when he stood up on his two legs. Judcote had found the monkey on the loose in Liverpool, but had never discovered how it had come to be in the port. There was some speculation that it had been brought in through the docks by a sailor and then abandoned.

What was strange about Hulch was his almost human eyes. Most primates have brown eyes, but Mr Judcote's monkey had very expressive eyes of a deep China blue. Anyway, on this day, the monkey swung down from the tree and watched its master in fascination as he drank the whiskey. Mr Judcote laughed and poured a shot for the monkey into a small porcelain teacup. The animal sniffed the cup, then put it to its lips and threw back its head – and drank it down in one go. It then clutched its throat and rolled comically across the lawn. Mr Judcote laughed at Hulch's antics, and the monkey loped off to chase a rabbit it had spotted at the bottom of the garden.

On the adjoining plot of land there was a smaller cottage, built by Mr Judcote for his former Liverpudlian maid, Mrs Hemmingway, and her family. Mrs Hemmingway had been recently widowed, and she was doing a very good job of rearing her seven-year-old son, her six-year-old daughter Clara, and her nine-month-old baby, Lizzie, who had been born on Duke Street and recently brought to Manxbridge.

On this hot July day, Clara was allowed to look after baby Lizzie, and she had dressed her in a pink, petal-rimmed bonnet and a little peach-coloured dress. She then walked into the garden, rocking the baby in her arms. From a tree across the field, Hulch watched Clara holding the infant, and out of curiosity perhaps, he nimbly ran down the tree and went over to them to get a closer look. Clara waved her finger at the monkey and told him he wasn't allowed in the garden. The monkey took no notice, and walked up to the girl and tried to snatch at the baby's dress. Clara ran inside the cottage and

shouted for her mother, but she had popped out to the shops in the local village. The door was slammed in the monkey's face, but it kept looking through the windows with an expression of utmost concern, as if it was worried about the baby. Clara and her brother laughed at his comical face at the window. But this was where events took a nasty turn.

About ten minutes later, Clara's older brother came out of the house with one of Clara's dolls, and he had deliberately dressed it in the baby's clothes. He had taken off Lizzie's bonnet and dress and put it on a doll. He then ran outside, and threw the doll up in the air, and laughed as he caught it, knowing that poor old Hulch would be tricked into thinking it was baby Lizzie. The monkey came screaming out of a hedge and Clara's brother ran inside the cottage, clutching the doll. He closed the door, and he and Clara fell about laughing as the monkey's frantic face peered in turn through each window.

Then, their mother returned, and as she entered the cottage with a basket full of groceries, Hulch barged past her, knocking the basket out of her hand. He seized Lizzie from her little bed, and ran back out of the cottage as Clara and her mother screamed. Hulch ran across a field of barley with the stunned baby cradled in his great, hairy arms. William Judcote was informed, and he summoned his seven servants, and they boarded two carriages to the village, while Judcote mounted his horse and rode like the devil after the baby-snatching monkey.

When he reached the village of Manxbridge, he found the place in turmoil with people running about excitedly. Then he saw, to his horror, that Hulch was crawling over the rooftops of the houses, still cradling Lizzie in his enormous arms. The baby appeared to be more bemused than afraid.

Villagers took up the chase wielding pitchforks, sticks, and even blunderbusses. One man fell and broke his legs as he tried to intercept the monkey on the roof. Hearts missed a beat as Hulch leapt across a wide gap between two roofs. Then they lost sight of him. People tried to comfort Mrs Hemmingway, but she was hysterical, and she severely scolded her children when a servant told her that he had seen them taunting the monkey.

Not long afterwards, Hulch appeared on top of a large chimney stack over the village inn – his long arms empty. Mrs Hemmingway fainted. The monkey was making a gibbering sound, as he gazed down at the sea of faces below. Faces filled with hatred now. Three villagers aimed their blunderbusses and an old flintlock at the monkey and fired a volley. Hulch fell backwards from the chimney and toppled down the back of the roof.

When the crowds surged to the back of the village inn, they found a trail of blood which led down a short dusty lane to a barn, where bales of hay and wool were stored. Inside the barn, near the door, lay the wounded animal, quivering with shock, with a gunshot wound in his shoulder. He started to crawl across the barn floor towards the bales of hay, and a villager aimed a blunderbuss down at the creature, but Mr Judcote, the monkey's owner stood in the way and begged him to hold fire. An argument ensued, but then everyone stopped talking when they heard the sounds of a baby crying.

Mr Judcote and the villagers peered over the stack of hay, and saw baby Lizzie, laying on a bale of wool, holding a large rosy apple. She was completely unharmed. Mr Judcote had the monkey taken back to his cottage, where he paid a physician to treat the animal, and he managed to save Hulch's life. Taking into consideration the fact that the monkey had thought he was rescuing Lizzie from harm on the day he snatched her, his life was spared, and he later became Lizzie's pet as she grew up.

The life expectancy of a chimpanzee is fifty years. Hulch lived for another eighteen years, but eventually became very grey and arthritic. He was allowed in the village church on the day that Lizzie Hemingway was married, and shortly afterwards, he went off to die in a woods.

NIXI

What follows is one of the strangest and yet highly intriguing tales I have ever researched. It all began one sunny spring morning in the early 1950s, on the rooftop playground of Windsor Street County School in south Liverpool. A quiet girl of almost thirteen years of age – who we shall call Emily – was skipping over the long rope being swung by her friends, when she caught a glimpse of something which fell from the clear blue sky and landed in a dark corner of the playground. At first Emily thought the object was a balloon, but when she went to take a closer look, she got the shock of her life. An alarming figure, about three feet in height, stood in the shadows. Its head was egg-shaped and green, and its eyes were bright purple. The unearthly entity stood there with a shy expression on its face and smiled coyly.

Emily immediately turned on her heels and ran off to tell her friends about the amazing creature, but when they rushed over to the corner, they found nothing. They called Emily a liar, as children do, and soon dispersed, but as soon as they went away to resume their games, the diminutive green man reappeared, smiling shyly as before.

Emily was a little scared, and she asked the extraordinary creature who he was. "My name is Nixi," said the peculiar-looking being, and he thrust out his hand, startling Emily. She couldn't bring herself to shake the little green man's hand, and instead ran to tell her friends that the 'thing' was back. This time when the playmates converged on the corner they saw nothing but a green, football-sized globe. As one of the children bent to pick up the globe, he was momentarily distracted by the teacher blowing a whistle to sound the end of the playtime period. The child then turned back to look at the ball but was mystified to find that it was gone.

Emily's mother, who is now eighty-four, related the rest of this bizarre story to me. Nixi apparently followed Emily home to her house on Gwendoline Street, because the child constantly claimed that the green, imp-like being had made himself at home in her bedroom. Emily's mother went up to investigate, but her daughter claimed that she was the only person who could see Nixi, except for Peggy, the family's elderly, grey-nosed, Welsh corgi. At first, Emily's mother naturally assumed that Nixi was merely a product of her child's overactive imagination, but Peggy's uncharacteristically timid behaviour made her think twice, because the dog absolutely refused to go into

Emily's bedroom. Also, Emily's mother could not help noticing the strange concepts and advanced words which her daughter began use to explain Nixi's presence "down here".

"Nixi is from the middle star in the handle of the Frying Pan constellation," Emily explained. "He came down here because he's lonely and bored. I love him, and if he has to go back home, I'll be very sad."

Emily also told her mother that Nixi could change his shape to mimic anything, and liked to play pranks on people. Apparently his weak spot was music, because whenever Emily played a tune on her recorder, Nixi would drift off into a deep, almost comatose, sleep. Nixi had also bragged that unlike humans, he never fell ill, or felt under the weather, and didn't require either water or food.

Alas, the fascinating visitor from elsewhere one day vanished after saying he missed his home, and Emily said that Nixi had taken her favourite book, *Anne of Green Gables* with him! Emily was inconsolable over the departure of her green friend for weeks.

In 1959, Emily married and moved to London. Today she reminisces over her enigmatic childhood friend, and insists he was not imaginary. If, as Emily claimed, Nixi came from Mizar – the middle star in the handle of the 'Frying Pan' constellation (Ursa Major) – he would have made a round trip of one hundred and sixty-two light years. I don't know what to make of the tale, but, as Shakespeare once wrote, 'There are more things in heaven and earth, than are dreamt of in our philosophy'.

NAZI TIMESLIP

A Merseyside man named Stuart reported the following strange and intriguing story to me in the summer of 2002. Stuart and his wife Kelly kept the story secret for years, but finally decided to call me at Radio Merseyside to relate the strange tale. This is their story:

In August 1996, Stuart, from Liverpool, made an appointment to see his doctor, as he was suffering from depression. The doctor suggested psychotherapy initially, but later prescribed Prozac because he came to believe that Stuart's depression was being caused by a chemical imbalance in his brain. Stuart's outlook on life picked up for a while, and in October of that year he decided to take his wife to London for a week, where they would stay at the home of his brother in Willesden.

Stuart and his wife Kelly enjoyed the visit, seeing the sights, going to a show, shopping, and spending time with his brother, but just before they were due to return to Liverpool, Stuart underwent a dramatic mood swing which left him in a very depressed state. He announced that he wanted to go abroad, to get away from the old familiar scenes in Liverpool. Kelly tried to talk him out of the idea, but Stuart was determined, so she had to telephone home and ask her daughter to post the passports, along with some extra clothes. Kelly assumed that they were going to Spain, and kept saying it would be a waste of money going there in October, but Stuart suddenly told her that he had booked a flight to the Channel Islands – they were going to Jersey.

They flew to the island of Jersey from Heathrow, and booked into a hotel. This is where events took a very strange turn. It was Halloween, and there was a fancy dress party at the hotel in which staff and entertainers dressed up as witches and ghosts. The party went on until eleven o'clock at night. Around this time, Stuart and Kelly decided to turn in for the night, and they walked up the stairs to their hotel room. As they were going down the corridor, all the wall lights became very dim, and the wallpaper turned dark. Stuart thought it was some spooky special effect which the management had laid on for Halloween – then they heard a woman screaming somewhere. Kelly grabbed Stuart by his arm and clung on to him, trembling. The screams came from behind a door on the left, a little further down the corridor. Stuart tried to open the door, and his wife begged him not to get involved. The door was locked, so Stuart pounded his fist on it. Then the door handle turned and the door swung open. A man stood there in a grey army uniform. The jacket of this uniform had a distinctive cloth badge of an eagle over the right breast pocket, and this eagle was perched on a swastika. The man standing before Stuart was dressed as a German officer. In the background, there was another man, partly dressed, and on a bed, Stuart could see a naked woman, and she was sobbing. Stuart surmised that the man in front of him was part of the Halloween fancy dress party from downstairs, but he gradually realised to his horror that this wasn't the case at all. The man said something in German, and walked back into the room as he closed the door behind him.

"Come on, Stuart. Let's not get involved," said Kelly. She pulled him away and they both walked down the corridor, when suddenly a voice shouted out behind them, "Kommen sie hier!" The couple turned to see the man in the Nazi uniform standing outside his hotel room – and he was pointing a pistol at them. Stuart recognised the make of the pistol. It was a Luger.

The German officer beckoned them with his hand to come to him, and as he did so, his friend emerged from the bedroom, buttoning up his jacket. The two Nazis spoke softly to each other in German, then the second man produced a pistol and he got behind Stuart and Kelly. He shunted them along the corridor, and Stuart said, "Okay the joke's over". He prayed it was all just a Halloween prank, but the men looked every bit the German soldier and seemed deadly serious. They were marched down the stairs to the first floor of the hotel, and then directed at gunpoint to a corridor, where two more men in outdated Nazi uniforms were standing, both of them enjoying cigars as they watched Stuart and Kelly approaching. The Liverpool couple were searched, and their passports and credit cards taken. They were then roughly pushed into a luxurious hotel suite, where a distinguished-looking white haired man of about sixty was sitting at a large desk. He too wore a grey uniform, and the officer who led the couple into the room saluted him. Standing before the chief German officer's desk was a British policeman, and Stuart said to him, "What's going on?" The British bobby looked stuck for words and somewhat afraid. The officer sitting at the desk gave a salute, and the British policeman returned the Nazi salute, then left.

The silvery-haired superior officer spoke good English and he asked the couple who they were as one of his men handed him the couple's passports and personal effects, which included a mobile phone. He scrutinised the credit cards with a look of fascination, then studied the passport with a look of utter disbelief. He kept remarking upon Stuart's year of birth, which was 1950, which according to the Nazi, was seven years away. Stuart quickly realised that this meant it was now somehow 1943. Then he noticed the calendar on the desk which stated it was Sunday 'Oktober' 31, 1943. Stuart and Kelly had somehow walked back fifty-three years into the past – back to the Jersey of 1943, which was occupied by the German army in World War Two.

Stuart afterwards said that he felt so afraid that he wanted to be physically sick. It was all too real to be a dream. Stuart told the German officer he was from Liverpool, as was his wife, and the officer kept looking at the passport and credit cards and the wallet full of strange-looking banknotes – banknotes that featured an unknown monarch. The officer walked to an old telephone and dialled a number on it, he talked excitedly into the mouthpiece in German as he held the mobile phone and Stuart and Kelly's passports.

All of a sudden, Stuart and Kelly found themselves in a cool, dark, silent room. Kelly stumbled about and found a light switch. She flicked it, and three long neon lights flickered to full illumination on the ceiling. They were in a kitchen of some sort. They went through a door and found themselves in the hotel corridor. They'd just come from the hotel's kitchen. The couple clung on to one another, and discussed the incredible events they had just experienced. They climbed up to the next floor and saw, with relief, that the corridor had reverted to its normal beige colour. The dim lights on the walls had vanished and the corridor was altogether brighter. Then Stuart looked at the clock in his room – it was four in the morning.

The next morning they told the manager the incredible tale, but he refused to believe them. However, the couple's passports were later found in a cupboard in the kitchen, although the credit cards were never found. Strangely, the mobile phone appeared out of thin air in the hotel car park, in front of two guests.

I investigated the case and showed Stuart a series of untitled photographs of German officers. He immediately picked out one. It was the photograph of General-Major Siegfried Heine, the Commander of Jersey in 1943. Stuart's wife independently picked out the same man.

I later discovered that General Major Heine had his headquarters at the very hotel where Stuart and Kelly had been staying. I also discovered that the civil police on Jersey continued to wear the usual British uniform during the Nazi Occupation, but they were required to salute German officers, or face a fine or punishment, so that would seem to explain why the policeman had saluted General Heine in his office.

I mentioned this case on the *Billy Butler Show* on Radio Merseyside, and a listener named Geoff from Halewood said that he had been to a hotel in Jersey in the early 1990s, and when he arrived, he was astonished to see a Nazi flag flying on a flagpole on top of the building. Geoff mentioned it to the receptionist, who denied there was such a flag flying. Geoff went outside with the receptionist and pointed up to – nothing! The flag had vanished, along with the flagpole.

Geoff slowly came to realise that he had somehow seen a flashback from the dark history of the island.

KILLED BY A DEAD MAN

In 1872, Henry Taylor, a sixty-six-year-old confidence trickster from Winsford in Cheshire, embezzled and swindled his way across England. He impersonated a policeman in Liverpool, and wormed his way into an old woman's house and conned her out of her life savings by telling her that he would put the money in a safe at the police station. Of course, the money was never seen again. Then the despicable Mr Taylor set up a bogus collection for the blind at Telford, before quickly vacating that town. He then turned up in Wolverhampton, claiming he could cure any ailment by using his hypnotic powers, but made the mistake of trying deceive the wife of a police sergeant with his latest scam, and narrowly escaped arrest.

Taylor subsequently fled to London, where he invented a new alias, introducing himself as Arthur Sexton. He moved into a lodging house in the Paddington area, and ingratiated himself with the landlady, a Mrs Williams, originally from Liverpool, who was looking after her sick seventy-five-year-old husband Archie. Archie Williams took an instant dislike to the new lodger, and told his wife there was something evil about the man. Mrs Williams felt that her husband had become isolated because of his illness, and assured him that the new lodger was a charming man with very good manners. However, Mrs Williams was soon to see Taylor in his true colours – literally – when he took off all his clothes one night and confronted her in the kitchen, saying that he wanted to make love to her. The woman screamed and warned him to leave alone, or she'd call the police. Mr Taylor returned partly clothed and begged Mrs Williams to let him stay. He explained that the landlady's beauty had overwhelmed him and made him act like a love-struck fool. He even managed to produce real tears as he knelt before the gullible landlady, clutching her apron and sobbing pitifully.

He must have given a very convincing performance, because Mrs Williams forgave him, and that night they talked until midnight, and she told him about her nagging worry that if her husband happened to die, she'd be terribly lonely. Very unwisely, she also disclosed that she stood to receive a substantial insurance payout, adding that it could never replace her dear husband Archie.

By a strange twist of fate, that very same night, Archie passed away as he slept beside his wife. After the tragedy – or stroke of good luck – as Henry

Taylor saw it, he stuck to the landlady like glue as he schemed up ways to relieve her of the insurance money. Wearing a long face, he attended the funeral service, then accompanied Mrs Williams to the place of burial, which was London's Kensal Green cemetery.

In the pouring rain, six pallbearers carefully manoevred the heavy lead-lined coffin from the funeral hearse, and then proceeded down the path, when suddenly, it became apparent that the pallbearer in front was obviously drunk. Horrified, the chief pallbearer ordered the man to get to the back of the coffin, and as the man did so, he slipped in the mud, and the coffin, being wet with rain, slipped and started to fall.

The widowed Mrs Williams screamed, and Henry Taylor rushed forward to try and get a grip of the heavy coffin, but he too slipped in the mud, fell on his back, and the end of the coffin crashed down on him, smashing straight into his Adam's apple and driving his bottom jaw into the roof of his mouth.

Slithering about in the mud, the pallbearers struggled to wrench the heavy oak coffin off Henry Taylor. As they did so, he instinctively put his hand to his face and pulled his shattered jaw apart, causing a communal shudder to pass through all the mourners. He was taken to hospital, but died minutes afterwards from the effects of traumatic shock. At the morgue, the police discovered his identity from various documents in his jacket, realising that the dead man was the callous confidence trickster who was wanted by police forces across the country. All sympathy for the victim of the freak accident evaporated, and the detectives agreed that it was a case of poetic justice and that Mrs Williams had had a very narrow escape.

LONG TALL SALLY

The following story was pieced together from the memories of several readers, including a policeman and a priest. Understandably, the relatives of the family mentioned in the story do not want to be identified, so I have had to change their surname.

In the early 1970s, a gang of six children from Spellow Lane, ranging in age from twelve to fifteen, used to play in Anfield cemetery. They would play hide and seek in the necropolis, and the older ones would court girls in the secluded setting. One evening in the September of 1973, two members of the gang, Tony and David, both aged fourteen, were in the Walton Lane end of the cemetery, when they saw a curious sight. A tall woman, dressed in a long black dress, and with a head of curly black hair, was kneeling in front of a gravestone, rubbing her hand across the inscription. Tony felt very nervous on this autumn night, because twilight was gathering, and a huge full moon was looming on the horizon. "Let's go, David," he said. "She looks weird."

David was a bit of a joker, and he smiled and said, "Nah, let's see what she's doing. She's round the twist – look."

The woman appeared to be rubbing soil into the surname part of the inscription on the gravestone. The boys moved in a bit further and hid behind a tree. They saw the woman stand up, and she looked abnormally tall, at least six-foot-four in height. She had a very pale face, and a long aquiline nose. Her eyes seemed very dark, as if she had put too much mascara on.

"*You* can stay if you like, but *I'm* going," said Tony. "She looks creepy."

And the child went to sneak away, but David shouted to the woman in black: "Hey, love!"

She slowly turned around and looked over at the boys with an expression of unadulterated hatred. She lifted her right hand in one swift movement, and they saw that she was wielding a long bladed carving knife. She muttered something unintelligible and started running towards them. Tony's legs turned to jelly. David ran off ahead of him and was soon leaping over the ivy covered wall. He glanced back and heard the woman shouting something in a deep, almost manly, voice. Her face too looked suspiciously masculine.

Tony just managed to get to the cemetery wall in time, and David grabbed his hand and pulled him up. The woman, or man, whatever it was, had hold of his right foot. Using all his strength, David pulled him free and the two of them dropped down the other side and ran off down Walton Lane. Halfway down the street, Tony realised that he was only wearing one shoe, the other must have been pulled off by the woman in black.

The story of the weird woman in the cemetery soon spread, and the local children nicknamed her Long Tall Sally because 'she' was said to be very lanky.

Days after the Sally scare broke out, two thirteen-year-old girls walking through the cemetery after dusk saw a woman dressed in black sitting on a gravestone, looking intently at the headstone. In her hand she held a long knife. The girls tiptoed past, then started to run as fast as their legs would carry them. Long Tall Sally started to give chase, and the girls just managed to escape in time, because the strange woman was never seen to leave the cemetery.

In the winter of 1974, a priest was visiting a grave late one afternoon, when he saw the woman in black sitting on a gravestone, gazing at a white marble headstone and he stopped to talk to her. He asked her why she was sitting there, and the woman said, "I should be buried there." She continued to stare intently at the white headstone, which was inscribed with the words, 'Matthew Deary and Jean Deary. Rest in peace'.

The priest could plainly see that the 'woman' was really a man wearing heavy make-up; the bright red lipstick and thick black mascara had been applied in a haphazard and heavy-handed fashion. His hands were huge and hairy – and as he surveyed the unmistakably male hands, he suddenly noticed the large knife which the man in drag was holding. The priest was nervous but he tried to compose himself and was able to say, "But you're not dead yet."

The man wearing a woman's wig turned, and his sad, bloodshot eyes were brimming with tears. "Oh! I am very dead," he said.

The priest realised that he was talking to a ghost, and he bravely recited a prayer on the spot for the troubled apparition. Shortly afterwards the figure is said to have slowly and peacefully dematerialised into the cool autumn air. The priest made inquiries locally and discovered that a man named Martin Benedict had been buried in the grave beneath that particular headstone. In the same grave was his Aunt Nora. Martin had been put in the care of his aunt because his parents, on discovering that he was homosexual, had rejected him. However, Martin was soon to find out that his aunt was not as broadminded as he had hoped.

One day she came home to find him dressed in the outfit she'd worn at a

42

recent funeral, complete with hat and shoes. He was also wearing one of his aunt's wigs and her lipstick. When she had sufficiently recovered from the shock, she told Martin that he looked ridiculous, and that he'd burn in hell because he was sick and twisted. He ran back to his parents, but they wouldn't even let him in the house. He must have felt doubly rejected because he was later found hanged at his Aunt Nora's house.

Everything started to make sense to the priest, because he had heard accounts from people who said that the ghost had been seen rubbing out the surname of the inscription which read 'Martin Benedict'. Martin's real named had been Martin Deary, and the grave he had been seen staring at so sorrowfully, had been that of his parents.

Tony, the boy who had his shoe pulled off by the apparition, is now a policeman in Liverpool, and whenever he drives past Anfield, he still experiences a cold shiver of fear.

THE SAD TALE OF MADGE KIRBY

In the back yard of a certain house on Underley Street, in the Edge Hill area of Liverpool, there is a dark, stubborn stain which is said to be the ingrained trace of a murdered child's blood. Many years ago, when my sister lived in this street, I was shown the stain. It is a dark, disc-shaped discolouration on the back step, about four inches in diameter. Local legend has it that it is the blood of Madge Kirby, a child who was abducted and killed in Edwardian times.

I first heard of the sad tale of Madge from my grandmother, Rose Slemen, when I was a child. I fondly recall the stormy afternoon I played truant and gallivanted up Crown Street, where I was collared by my grandmother. She told me that I could have been snatched by a stranger, and I, being morbidly curious, went to her home in Myrtle Gardens, eagerly asking what might have happened to me had I been picked up by a stranger. When I reached my gran's home, she told me the following true story.

The sad tale of Madge Kirby began at 4.30pm on the dark wintry afternoon of Monday, 6 January 1908. Seven-year-old Margaret Kirby, known affectionately as Madge by her father and friends, was playing near the reservoir in Farnworth Street, Kensington, just around the corner from her home at Number 55 Romily Street. Her father David, thirty-eight, was a plumber, but work had been slow because of his severe depression, caused by the loss of his wife, who had died from a long illness, just a fortnight before during the Christmas period.

On that cold afternoon in 1908, as twilight gathered, a man in black clothes approached Madge, who was playing in the street with her best friend Annie McGovern.

"Would you like to go with me for some sweets?" the stranger asked in a well-spoken voice. He had probably chosen her because she was said to have been a child who always stood out amongst her peers because of her beauty.

Madge nodded, and the sinister man in black took her by the hand and walked her away into the wintry murk. When Madge did not return home for her tea, her father went in search of her, without success. He listened with dread when young Annie and several other children told him about the man who had accosted Madge with a promise of sweets – the classic approach of the paedophile.

The police lost no time in launching a wide-scale search party for the missing girl. Lakes were dragged, parks scoured, over five thousand empty houses were searched, and there were door-to-door enquiries in Kensington and parts of Edge Hill, but Madge could not be found. Mr Kirby was devastated by his daughter's abduction, and his sisters and his three-year-old son could only provide only a modicum of consolation for him. The police asked him for a detailed description of his missing daughter, to be circulated to police stations throughout Lancashire. Fighting back stinging tears, David told them that Madge had been wearing a black shirt with worn sleeves, a blue pinafore, a black velvet bonnet with black strings, black stockings and laced boots. His beloved daughter had brown hair, sky-blue eyes and a very fair and fresh-faced complexion.

In St Michael's School, which Madge Kirby had attended, the teachers and children said a prayer each day for the missing girl's safe return. The months wore on, but still no trace of Madge could be found – until eight months later, on the morning of Tuesday 21 August, when a man going to work came upon a dirty old onion sack, outside a condemned house on Great Newton Street, off London Road. That sack contained the remains of a scantily-clad girl. The body of Madge Kirby had been found at last. Now the hunt was on for her killer.

Detectives were intrigued as to how the onion sack containing Madge's remains had been dry, while the pavement was wet from a recent rainfall. A subsequent investigation determined that the sack had been kept in the cellar of the derelict house. The police lost no time in launching a murder hunt, but their investigations were hampered by the public, large numbers of whom congregated outside the Prescot Street police station, waiting and watching for any new developments in the shocking murder case.

On the night after the body was found, two policemen rushed out of the police station with a bloodhound leading the way. The dog led the officers in a westerly direction, and the great mob followed – six raced after the police on bicycles, two elderly men were pushed along in their wheelchairs, and several women even pushed prams containing their infant children as they joined the hunt. Over two thousand people poured down Prescot Street, many of them carrying refreshments, towards the city centre, but little did they know that the bloodhound they were following, impressive though it was, was but a decoy.

Shortly after midnight, one of the most sensitive bloodhounds ever deployed by the Lancashire Constabulary emerged from the police station and immediately took up the faded but still useable scent he'd taken from the clothes of the murdered child. The dog's name was Czar, and he had been loaned from a dog-handler named Mr Pakenham. Czar took the police on a curious meandering trail that wound through the Botanic Gardens, then on to a strip of secluded wasteground on the eastern extremities of Edge Lane. From there, Czar led the constables to Tunnel Road, and on to Edge Hill railway station. In an unusually excited state, Czar dragged the policeman to the city centre-bound platform and stood stock still, gazing at the tunnel. He convulsed, and sniffed the air. That tunnel led to Lime Street.

Czar was bundled into a cab, and the taxi driver was instructed to go to Lime Street station, where the bloodhound bolted for platform one. Czar barked and howled at the tunnel, and the dog's owner took that to mean that Madge Kirby's killer had left Liverpool for the Midlands, as trains from that platform were bound for the metropolis of Birmingham. There, the tantalising trail went cold.

Police received a letter, purportedly from the child killer, which stated that the murderer had once lived as a lodger on the premises where the body was found, and that he had kept the key, so that he would have access to the empty house. He said he'd taken Madge to the derelict house, where he had sadistically killed her. Eight months later he had decided to 'let the world know' what had become of Madge Kirby, so he dragged her badly-decomposed remains from the cellar of the house on Great Newton Street and placed them in the onion sack which was then left on the pavement. The mystery then deepened when several people came forward and told police that they had spotted a sinister man, dressed as a woman, climbing over the back yard wall of the empty house on Great Newton Street on the morning the body was found in the bag. Police later suspected a man named Thompson who had lodged in Great Newton Street, but they were never able to track him down.

Madge's heartbroken father never recovered from the murder, and died weeks after his beloved daughter's body was found. Today, Madge Kirby lies at rest in Ford cemetery, the forgotten victim of an Edwardian child-killer. Which grave in Liverpool, or perhaps Birmingham, contains the remains of Madge Kirby's murderer? A rumour persisted that the killer lived on Underley Street, and that he had been responsible for several attacks on children and young women in the alleyways off Smithdown Road in 1907, months before the Kirby outrage. Some said he was a sailor, others maintained that the sex attacker had the appearance of a clerk.

Perhaps the psychopathic paedophile worked at Edge Hill railway station. That would account for the bloodhound Czar's erratic behaviour at the railway tunnels of Edge Hill and Lime Street. Perhaps the killer hadn't fled to another city at all – perhaps he worked on those railway lines, as a signalman, a railway goods inspector, or a porter. He only had to take the child through the gaslit streets of Kensington via a direct route to the murder scene: from Edge Hill station to Lime Street, where he could disembark and walk the short distance to Great Newton Street.

The killer escaped the black cap and cheated the hangman, and now lies mouldering in his grave, but perhaps his troubled, remorse-filled spirit wanders the night, revisiting the scenes of his heinous crimes. Over the years, a shadowy man in black has been seen walking silently up Romily Street and Jubilee Drive with his head bowed. The consensus of the older folks residing in the area of the haunting in the 1950s was that the dark apparition was the restless earthbound shade of Madge Kirby's killer, retracing each step of his prowling itinerary of long ago, whilst dreading the arrival of the Highest Judge of all – on Judgement Day.

LOVING MEMORY

One snowy January afternoon in 1877, Alfred Roddy, a sixty-nine-year-old shopkeeper, locked up his Dale Street shop earlier than usual – at about four o'clock – and began to walk home to his house near to where the Churchill Way Flyover is now situated, close to Crosshall Street. Mr Roddy was a widower who had something of a lonely existence. He had lived on his own since the death of his wife ten years before, and even though he had been very fond of her when she was alive, he had only truly loved one woman in his life, when he was forty.

The one who he had loved but lost, had been a poor girl from Everton called Hannah Cordwainer. She had been only eighteen but he had fallen in love with her from the moment he had set eyes upon her, and she had regarded him in the same way.

Unfortunately, Hannah was very impoverished, and Alfred Roddy's father had pressured him into marrying a woman nearer to his own age, Agnes Black, the daughter of a wealthy businessman. To make matters worse, young Hannah's Catholic father had threatened to disown her if she married a Protestant such as Alfred Roddy. Hannah was forbidden to go near Alfred, and Alfred's father and Agnes Black's parents forced Alfred Roddy to give up his love for Hannah. That was twenty-nine years before, in 1843. Now, at the age of sixty-nine, Alfred realised just how much love he felt for Hannah, because in most people, the passing of time quickly dilutes the love between couples, but almost thirty years on, Alfred Roddy still dreamt of Hannah Cordwainer, and when he drank his whisky nightcap at the sentimental hour of midnight, he tortured himself with thoughts of what might have been.

On this snowy afternoon, he was lost in such thoughts about Hannah when he was knocked down on the frosted cobbled road by a wagon. The horse had bolted out of control, and as the driver struggled to regain control, people rushed to Mr Roddy's aid. He was taken to his home, where a doctor treated him. He had only suffered a few minor cuts and bruises, but during the fall he had hit his head on the cobblestones, and the concussion had left him with severe amnesia. He didn't even know his own name. A neighbour offered to look after him at his home, as he didn't have any relatives she knew of, and the doctor said he would call each day to ascertain how serious the head injury was.

Alfred Roddy was put to bed, and his neighbour Mrs Campbell kindly looked after him. His amnesia showed no signs of lifting after a week, and Mrs Campbell became very weary, because she also had her own family to look after. One day she asked the friend of a cousin to help out, and the woman duly arrived at the house. This helper was a pretty forty-nine-year-old woman, and Alfred Roddy became very animated when he saw her. He told her she had beautiful eyes, and suddenly, the woman gasped in astonishment. Turning to Mrs Campbell, the woman inquired, "Is this man's name Alfred Roddy?"

Mrs Campbell said it was, and the woman, whose name was Hannah Cordwainer, whispered that she had once been in love with him, almost thirty years before. Hannah sat on Alfred's bed and he held her hand. He said, "I don't know who you are, and yet I love you. Did I once know you?"

Hannah found herself falling back in love with Alfred Roddy, and Alfred Roddy was falling in love with the woman who had been the one true love of his life – all over again.

As soon as Hannah revealed her name, Alfred gazed at her in total astonishment, and tears started to fall from his eyes. "Why do I cry?" he asked. "You must have been close to my heart. Are you my wife?"

Hannah became tearful too, and she kissed Alfred. He suddenly muttered one word – "Hannah". The fog of amnesia had blotted out all of the details of Alfred Roddy's life, but it had been unable to erase his cherished memories of Hannah.

Gradually, Alfred's memory returned, and he and Hannah were married that July.

THE DANCING DRESS

On the Wednesday night of 12 April 1978, Graham, from Crosby, was in a Liverpool pub in Williamson Square, celebrating Liverpool's three-nil victory over Borussia Moenchengladbach. During the celebrations, Graham noticed an attractive red-headed woman of about thirty, sitting at the bar with some friends. Being slightly intoxicated, and full of Dutch courage, he swaggered over to the woman and asked if he could buy her a drink. She politely replied, "No thanks," and continued her conversation. The last orders bell was rung, and over the clamour and hubbub of the drinkers, the barman called, "Come on now, drink up."

Graham thought the redhead was the most beautiful woman he'd seen in years, and he felt compelled to let her know about his amorous feelings. He overheard her saying to her friends that she'd be there on Saturday, before going on to Mr Pickwick's nightclub. Graham went home that night to Crosby, and on Saturday evening he was so eager to see the red-haired beauty again, that he persuaded a friend to drive him to Liverpool, where he was dropped off in Dawson Street, close to Williamson Square. He walked over to the pub where he had met the woman of his dreams and pushed open the door. His eyes quickly scanned the line of drinkers. His heart skipped a beat when he saw her sitting on a bar-stool. She looked absolutely sensational in a low cut top with her hair swept up in an elegant bun. Graham walked over to her, and saw that she was finishing off a glass of Baileys, so he ordered one for her, and when he placed the drink in front of her, he said: "You look absolutely beautiful."

The redhead smiled, whispered "Thanks", and as she sipped the Baileys they started to talk, and he discovered that her name was Cathy. She had just come out of a relationship and was in no hurry to begin another one just yet. Graham said he was single, and had also finished a long-term relationship a while back. He'd been with Philomena for seven years, but she'd left him for someone else exactly a year ago, in April. Cathy and Graham seemed to get on well, and he ended up taking his beautiful acquaintance to a club called the Silver Sands.

At about one o'clock that morning, the DJ put on a record for a slow dance, but instead of taking Cathy in his arms and dancing with her, Graham became very nervous. The number on the turntable was *Chanson D'Amour* by The Manhattan Transfer. The song had been a number one hit a year ago, which surprised a lot of people because it was an old song that had previously been recorded in 1961. Cathy noticed that Graham reacted rather strangely immediately the song was played. With a look of dread in his eyes, he pulled her out of the club and on to the cold and windy street. Cathy protested that she had left her coat behind in the club, but Graham prevented her from going back in to the Silver Sands. He said he knew the owner of the club, and promised he'd collect her coat in the morning. When Cathy persisted in trying to return to the nightclub, he hailed a taxi, and almost pushed his new girlfriend into the vehicle. The cab took them to Graham's home on Winchester Avenue in Crosby. Cathy kept asking Graham why he had left the club in such a hurry, and he seemed stuck for an answer. Despite having some misgivings about his behaviour, she was strongly attracted to Graham and that night they slept together, and later started going steady.

The relationship progressed, and one Saturday morning, at around three o'clock, she was lying next to him in bed. They had just returned from a night out at a club and Cathy had been so tired that she had flung her new scarlet dress over a chair in the bedroom and fallen into bed. Graham was already fast asleep, but once in bed, she suddenly felt wide awake and lit up a cigarette. She reached over to the clock radio and switched it on, but switched off the bedside lamp, because there was enough light shining into the room from a lamp-post outside. She carefully adjusted the volume so that it wouldn't wake Graham and then adjusted the tuner, searching for some suitable music to relax to, and the faint sounds of a melodic song came drifting in on Radio Luxembourg. The song on the radio was *Chanson D'Amour*.

As the song played, Cathy detected a rich, sweet-scented aroma in the air. A few moments later, she watched as her discarded dress rose up off the chair – as if some invisible figure was inside it. The gaudy garment made a dancing movement in time to the music, and twirled around as it waltzed across the bedroom. Cathy let out a scream that not only sent Graham flying out of bed, but brought the next-door neighbours hurrying to his front door. Graham grabbed the clock radio and switched it off, then clicked on the bedside lamp.

Where was Cathy? He found her in a terrible state downstairs, wearing one of his shirts. She told him to fetch a pair of jeans, as she was certainly never going to wear the red dress again. Graham told her to calm down and insisted she'd had a nightmare, but Cathy knew she had not been dreaming. She was very badly shaken and refused to go back to bed, and ordered Graham to take her home at once.

"This *is* your home isn't it?" was his reply.

"Not any more," said Cathy, and she warned him that she would get a cab home if he refused to drive her.

Graham pointed out that he couldn't legally drive as he'd been drinking at the club, so Cathy telephoned her brother-in-law and he came to pick her up. Graham begged her to stay, but she flatly refused – she was terrified of anything to do with the world of the supernatural and the dancing dress was too much for her. She said that her intuition told her that somehow Graham had something to do with the ghostly goings-on, at which Graham seemed stuck for words.

After that night Cathy stopped seeing him.

Graham died in 1980, and Cathy later heard a strange rumour.

In 1977, Graham was supposed to marry his long-term girlfriend, but she was diagnosed with breast cancer, and had tragically died before the wedding date. *Chanson D'Amour* had been her favourite song, and it was to have been played at the wedding. On her deathbed Graham had promised that he would never love another.

Months after the death of his girlfriend, Graham was intimately holding hands with a girlfriend across a table in a bistro. The strains of an instrumental version of *Chanson D'Amour*, played from the loudspeakers on the premises – when suddenly, the glass containing Graham's drink shattered, spraying him and his companion with wine and razor-sharp shards of glass. From that time onwards, Graham felt that the spirit of the girl he'd been untrue to was being conjured up every time he heard her favourite song – *Chanson D'Amour*, and this explained the mystery of the dancing dress.

POLLY

In Liverpool's Rodney Street, there is a very old dwelling that was once a nursing home which closed its doors for good a few years ago. Around the mid-1970s, a spate of ghostly activity broke out at the nursing home, and one of the first people to witness the supernatural goings-on was the matron, but she chose to say nothing at first, for fear of alarming the staff and patients.

However, a young nurse called Brenda was working on the nightshift one January evening at eleven o'clock, when she heard the sounds of what seemed to be a woman sobbing somewhere in the upper floors of the house. At first, Brenda thought it was a patient, but then she heard the dull footfall of someone coming down the stairs. Waiting in suspense at the foot of the stairs, Brenda saw the crying woman reach the landing above and turn to face her as she came down the staircase.

The woman was dressed from head to toe in white, and was aged between twenty and twenty-five years of age. The long, white, featureless garment was like an old-fashioned night-gown. Brenda's heart pounded, because the woman was partly transparent, and not only was her face as pale as chalk, there were two dark lines across her wrists, and blood was flowing copiously from the gashes. The phantom's ethereal cheeks glistened as tears flowed from a pair of large, black, sorrowful eyes. Brenda suddenly realised that the 'night-gown' was almost certainly a burial shroud.

Filled with a rising sensation of terror, the nurse turned, and found herself running down the stairs, unable to cry out. The ghost followed her down, and Brenda fled into the dark empty office that was occupied by the matron during the day. The nurse was so petrified that she slammed the door and hid under the desk, and listened in dread as the sounds of sobbing got nearer and nearer. The ghost came straight through the closed door, and walked towards the desk. The apparition was so vivid that Brenda could clearly see its bare, ashen feet standing by the desk. She screwed her eyes tightly shut and fervently made the sign of the cross – and when she opened them, the ghost had vanished. When she was sure that the ghost had finally gone, she switched on every light in the building and alerted two other nurses. That night, the three of nurses on duty were so frightened, they even refused to go to the toilet alone.

The next day, Brenda told the matron about the woman in white with the slashed wrists, expecting her superior to be sceptical. To her surprise, the matron said that she had also seen the woman in white at the nursing home – exactly three years before, on the 9 January. The matron said that she had always been a bit psychic, but had never told anyone about her gift, for fear of being ridiculed. When she had seen the spectre coming down the stairs, she had received the strong impression that the troubled ghost's name was Polly. Matron had also experienced an overpowering feeling of a sorrow which made her throat close up. Then, seconds afterwards, the wraith-like woman melted away.

Rather than putting her mind at rest, this new information made Brenda feel even more uneasy, because it confirmed that the nursing home was haunted, and therefore she could be confronted by the ghostly woman at any time. News of the haunting spread through the home and beyond, and one of the cleaners who had worked there in the past said that she had once seen the vivid ghost of a nun walking up the same stairs with her back to her.

From that day, Brenda refused point blank to do night shifts, and even during the day her nerves remained taut while she was on duty.

Around this time, Brenda started dating John David, whose unusual hobby was ghost hunting. He possessed all the equipment for this unusual pastime, and he often worked with a medium named Bill Holroyd, an epileptic young man who had quite a reputation for 'empathising' with ghosts. Unlike most mediums, Holroyd refused to be paid for a gift which he claimed had been given to him by "a higher authority".

Naturally, Brenda's boyfriend was fascinated by her encounter with the woman in white, and constantly asked her if he could investigate the case. She said he'd have to check with the matron. The matron refused his request at first, but later relented, when the ghost continued to make alarming appearances at the home. The matron said John and his mediumistic associate would be allowed a few hours, on the condition that they kept a low profile, and promised not to talk to anyone from the newspapers. John and Bill gave their word that they wouldn't seek any media attention.

About a week later, just before midnight, Bill warned the three nurses on night duty to stay in their staffroom. The ghost was about to walk, he told them, and he was right. First came the crying sound – then the pale, pathetic figure descended the stairs. John waited with a camera loaded with infra red film halfway up the stairs. He clicked on his audio cassette recorder. Bill Holroyd bravely intercepted the ghost on the stairs, wondering if it would walk right through him, but the ghost halted and gazed at him with a look of indescribable anguish. Bill whispered to her – questions about her name, and why she was so restless. Almost four minutes elapsed, and during that eternity of heightened suspense, John saw the girl's mouth faintly flicker. Then she slowly faded away, and Bill reached out slowly to touch the air where she had stood.

The medium came downstairs and imparted all of the information he had received from the ghost. Her name was Mary Burrows, but she had been known as Polly to her family and friends. She had lived locally in Falkner Square with her sisters and father and she had been deeply in love with a poor carpenter named Samuel. Polly had become pregnant with his child, and her father had been so outraged, that he had Samuel dragged into a solicitor's office, where he signed a contract which stipulated that he would receive a large sum of money if he would stop seeing Polly.

Samuel had chosen the money instead of Polly.

Having a child out of wedlock was regarded as scandalous in Victorian times, and Polly was locked away in a convent in the care of the nuns. After the birth, the nuns gave the baby away to a childless couple. Polly was convinced that Samuel would come and rescue her, but after months of waiting, she realised that he no longer cared for her, and in utter despair she slashed her wrists.

All of this information was checked and verified. The electoral registers were examined, and it was established that in Victorian times nuns did indeed run a home for unmarried mothers at the Rodney Street house which was presently occupied by the nursing home.

Further research ascertained that a Burrows family had lived in Falkner Square during that period. The medium spent almost a week at the nursing home, trying his utmost to persuade the tormented spirit of Polly Burrows to go to the world of peaceful spirits where she belonged, but she refused, and as far as I know, Polly still haunts the house on Rodney Street where she took her life in a moment of intense heartache.

THE GHOST OF STRAWBERRY FIELDS

Strawberry Fields, an orphanage on Beaconsfield Road in the Woolton district of Liverpool, is known across the world, as it is the subject of the famous Beatles song. The Salvation Army orphanage was founded in 1936, and in the following year a strange incident took place in its vicinity.

In December 1937, seven-year-old Elsie from Liverpool lost her mother to cancer. Her father had died years before, when Elsie was four. The girl was temporarily placed in the care of the Strawberry Fields orphanage three days before Christmas, until the authorities could find a suitable long term placement for the girl.

On the dark snowy morning of Christmas Eve, Elsie lay in her bed, overcome with loneliness and grief. She rose from her little bed and decided to write a letter to Father Christmas, asking him if he could leave her a baby brother. She found a pen and paper, and after she had written the note, she folded it and put on her coat and beret. The child somehow managed to sneak out of the grounds of the orphanage without being seen, to wander off in search of a post office pillar-box. She soon located what she was looking for and, filled with childish optimism, she posted her note. Her intention was to go straight back to Strawberry Fields, but somehow she lost her way.

Elsie trudged through the snow, down a lane off Yew Tree Road, where she came upon a cottage. Outside, in the garden, stood a snowman wearing a top hat. Elsie glanced through the window of this cottage and saw a scene which made her heart burn with sorrow and envy. A woman in a long pink dress was surrounded by a circle of laughing young girls and boys, holding hands as they danced around her. In the background stood a beautifully decorated Christmas tree. Green and red garlands and colourful paper decorations hung from the ceilings. The ring of children broke up, and one of them, a little boy with chestnut-coloured hair, looked up at the window and caught sight of

Elsie's sad face pressed against the pane. He drew the woman in pink's attention to Elsie's presence, and she quickly went outside to find the child.

Anxious that she was in for a telling-off, Elsie sneaked away and tried to hide behind the top-hatted snowman, but the woman soon found her, and leant forward. She smiled. "Good morning, child," she said, warmly. Elsie said she was lost, and the woman took her inside the cottage where she was introduced to the children and given a seat before the welcoming hearthside by a blazing fire. She was invited to join in the children's games, and afterwards she sat at a long table and enjoyed a hearty breakfast, followed by Christmas pudding and cake.

Sometime later, a grandfather clock struck the hour of eight o'clock as the pale light of morning filtered through the windows. The lady in the pink dress put on a long coat and a large white bonnet decked with flowers, then took Elsie by the hand. She took her out of the cottage as the children frowned and said their goodbyes to the orphan. Elsie looked back at the end of the path, and watched the children waving from the window and the hallway. She wished she could have stayed with them, as she hadn't a friend in the world.

The little orphan was led to the gates of Strawberry Fields, at which point the woman vanished after hugging her. Elsie ran into the orphanage and related her account of the kind lady and the children at "the lovely cottage". One of the musicians in the Salvation Army band was intrigued by the Yuletide mystery, and went in search of the cottage with Elsie on Christmas Day, but was unable to find the dwelling.

One day, in January 1938, a woman arrived at the orphanage to claim Elsie. It was an Aunt Julia she did not know of from Wigan; her father's sister. Elsie was delighted to go and live with Julia, who was heavily pregnant. When she gave birth to a son not long afterwards, Elsie wept with joy, for now she had a baby 'brother' to look after – Father Christmas had made her dream come true!

I mentioned this enchanting tale on the radio one afternoon and several elderly listeners from the districts of Allerton and Calderstones said they had been told by their parents that a young lady from a well-to-do family had once lived somewhere off Yew Tree Road in Victorian times. According to folklore, the lady had lost her husband in tragic circumstances, and adopted many underprivileged and abandoned children into her home, which was said to have been a large thatched cottage.

BAFFLING BIRTH

In Liverpool, in 1920, three sisters from Parliament Street with the surname Boole went to the Dragon Vaults public house, which once stood on Brownlow Hill. At the pub, Alice, Peggy and Margaret Boole, aged twenty-two, twenty and nineteen, had come to join their father, who was enjoying a drink with his seafaring brother. It was a family affair, and many other members of the Boole family were at the pub that afternoon. There were also three young men present: William Hunter, John Lewis and James Bruce. The men were soon chatting to the lovely Boole sisters.

Not long afterwards, William Hunter started seeing Alice Boole, John Lewis started to court Peggy Boole, and James Bruce later became engaged to Margaret Boole. James Bruce, who was of Scottish descent, stood out because his hair was of a very unusual shade of Titian red. All three were married on the same day that summer, and the landlady of the Dragon Vaults, Mrs Jessie Laycock, attended the triple wedding.

By 1922, Alice Boole – who was now Alice Hunter, and Peggy Lewis, her sister, had become mothers, but their younger sister Margaret and her husband James Bruce had still not produced a child, and Margaret yearned for a baby. In November 1922, the three husbands boarded the Cunard liner *Laconia* at the Pier Head to sail on her to New York, where the men would hopefully find employment, and set up homes in America for their wives to live in.

The three men felt mixed emotions as they waved goodbye to their wives from the deck of the ship – were they doing the right thing? And would they be able to build a better life for their families among the towering skyscrapers of New York?

It was one of those skyscrapers which was to claim the life of James Bruce, just one month later. Alice and Peggy heard the news first and had the unenviable task of breaking it to their little sister. With tears in their eyes they knocked on her door and when they had sat her down and made her a cup of tea, they told her that James had been killed in a freak accident on a construction site in New York. Margaret collapsed with the shock. When she came to, she locked herself away in her room and became a recluse, only seeing close members of her family when they came to visit her. She would clutch at her sister's baby daughter and start to sob, bemoaning the fact that she would never have a child of her own.

One stormy evening, Margaret ventured out of the house on Parliament Street and wandered aimlessly up Stanhope Street. As she was passing an old Methodist Chapel, a man appeared out of nowhere in front of her, startling her. His dark clothes looked very outdated. He gently took hold of her hand and asked her why she was so troubled. As he listened, he led her into the chapel, where he comforted the distressed young lady.

"Don't ever give up, a child may come."

Margaret turned around and found herself alone. The oddly dressed man with the kind face and the soft voice, had seemingly vanished into thin air. At that moment Margaret was suddenly transfused with an overwhelming sense of peace and optimism.

A month later, Margaret suddenly felt very poorly and a doctor was called out to examine her. The doctor stunned both her and her sisters, and the rest of the family, because he told Margaret Bruce that she was pregnant. Margaret dismissed the diagnosis as nonsense, as it was thirteen months since she had slept with her late husband. Nevertheless, the doctor insisted that she *was* pregnant. Bewildered, Margaret decided to get a second opinion, and the next doctor confirmed that she was indeed pregnant.

Nine months later, Margaret gave birth to a healthy baby daughter who was born with a full head of red hair, and her curly locks were of the same unusual shade as James Bruce – Titian red. News of the strange birth was viciously contested by Bishop Chavasse of Liverpool, but Margaret's friends and family backed up her testimony, testifying that the girl had spent the last thirteen months in self-imposed isolation in her own room, in a depressed state.

To her dying day, Margaret Bruce was convinced that the man she had met on Stanhope Street had been an angel – an angel who gave her the one thing she most wanted in the world – apart from her dead husband – a child of her own.

THE STRATEGIC RESERVE

I recall the night I was sleeping over at a school friend's house on Smithdown Lane in the 1970s, when I heard a dull thudding sound that gently shook the entire dwelling. From the top of the double bunk-bed I leant over and asked what had caused the jolt. My friend seemed as startled as I was, and he switched on the light and said that his father had told him that there were tunnels running under Smithdown Lane which were haunted by a ghostly steam train, which could make the house shake.

At that time, my friend was unaware of the amazing subterranean legacy of Joseph 'Mad Mole' Williamson, an eccentric from a bygone age who had riddled the sandstone bedrock of my Edge Hill neighbourhood with a system of tunnels which had no obvious purpose. I'd read about his labyrinth in the books of Richard Whittington Egan, and so I gradually drifted off into an uneasy sleep with imaginings of a secret city beneath the streets, populated by Victorians who had refused to die.

On the following morning over breakfast, I mentioned the mysterious house-jarring jolt in the night, and all conversation at the table instantly ceased. "That'll have been that ghost train I told you about," my friend's father eventually said. Nothing more was said on the subject, and to this day I do not know what rocked the house on Smithdown Lane. Surely, it could not really have been a ghostly steam train? Or could it?

Well, curiously, in recent years, the following tale came my way via the many telephone calls, emails and letters I receive in response to my broadcasts on Radio Merseyside. Had the story originated from just one source, I'd have taken it with a pinch of salt, but this account is the amalgamation of four separate people's correspondence. You may make of it what you will.

In March 1977, Tony Corbett, a scrap metal merchant was sitting in a café in Sayers, in Myrtle Parade, near the University campus. He was having a lunch break after buying a bundle of lead pipes from a man in the area. While eating his egg, beans and bacon, he thumbed through the pages of the *Daily Post* lying next to his plate, and glanced at the racing page. After a while he turned back a few pages to look at the television guide, when he happened to see a photograph of a white-haired man of about seventy-something in the corner of a page. The headline under the photo read: 'Have You Seen This Man?' The article named the man, and said he had walked out of an old people's home, and that relatives were worried about him. Tony Corbett flipped past the page and happened to look up – and there was the very same old man sitting at the next table – staring at a cup of tea with a pensive look on his face. As Tony watched him, the pensioner slyly took out a small bottle of purple methylated spirits, and secretively took a sip, then stashed the bottle away in his inside pocket. Tony approached the man, and pointed to his photograph in the newspaper. The old man read the article, then explained that he had decided to leave the home because he was bored stiff by the stultifying routine and lack of conversation. Mr Corbett advised him to at least telephone his relatives to put their minds at rest, but instead, the pensioner let out a string of expletives and claimed that his next of kin were hoping he'd die, so they could get their hands on his money.

Corbett and the elderly man got talking, and the scrap dealer complained that he was finding it impossible to make a living and his business was steadily folding. The old man seemed lost in thought for a while, then made a curious comment. "Do you own that scrap-yard by Crown Street?" he asked. Corbett nodded. The old man confided that he knew of an amazing secret connected with that yard which could net Mr Corbett a small fortune. Corbett's ears pricked up and he eagerly asked what the secret was, but the old man asked him to take him to the yard first.

Corbett had no hesitation in taking him, even though he was rather sceptical about the outcome, and when they reached the yard, the old man scurried behind a stack of rusting car chassis and inspected a heavy iron door. The door had been there for years, and Corbett had assumed that it provided access to the electrical transformer shed next door. The old man asked for a wire coat-hanger, and Corbett eventually located one. The old man carefully inserted the coat hanger's hook into the old padlock on the iron door, and gently twisted and manipulated it for about a minute.

Suddenly, the padlock clicked, and the old man deftly removed it – he'd obviously done this before – and Corbett wondered what he'd got himself involved in. The old man tried to pull open the door, but it wouldn't budge because the hinges were so badly rusted and he was quite frail. Tony Corbett, being very muscular, did manage to open the door. Beyond the doorway, a stone stairway descended into the darkness. The old man reached in and pressed a rubber-coated switch on the wall, and a line of bulbs behind wire-framed guards lit up the stairway.

"Wait till you see this, son," he said, and started to walk down the sandstone steps.

Corbett followed him, wondering where the steps led. After descending about five flights of steps, the two men walked down a corridor carved out of sandstone, and came upon an extraordinary sight. It looked like a deserted railway platform from long ago. Lined up on the tracks were three old steam locomotives, each in pristine condition.

"Phew! Thank goodness they're still here," he exclaimed.

He told Corbett that he had found the trains by accident about eleven years before, when he was a petty criminal, hiding stolen goods. Corbett asked him who the trains belonged to, and the old man shrugged. Perhaps the railway companies had forgotten about them, or simply left them there, he speculated.

Corbett knew a little about trains, and he saw that the large locomotive in front of him belonged to the same class as the Flying Scotsman. It bore the letters 'LNER' on its iron plating and also had a four-digit registration number on display. The second train was a turbomotive with the abbreviation 'LMS' upon it. The two men even climbed on board the engines, and saw that they looked and felt brand new.

About forty minutes later, the two men climbed back up to the scrap-yard. scrap-dealer spoke to a solicitor friend later that day and asked him if he could claim the trains as salvage, but the legal expert said that he couldn't, as they were the property of the railways, so he'd have to come clean and tell the authorities. The museums would probably purchase them.

However, a strange thing happened. Government officials descended upon the scene and cordoned off the scrap-yard. After interrogating Corbett at length, they said they were something to do with the Ministry of Defence, and told him to say nothing about his discovery. But the story got out anyway, and in several editions of a steam railway magazine, articles on the amazing story were printed. It transpired that the serial numbers of the secret locomotives were those of steam trains that had apparently not been scrapped. It was claimed that the Government had hidden away over a hundred locomotives and other transport vehicles in underground vaults and tunnels as part of a 'Strategic Reserve'. In the event of a serious crisis, like the aftermath of an atomic war, the coal mines would re-open, and these primitive vehicles would be brought back into operation. It was alleged that the Ministry of Defence even admitted to all this in 1979.

When a nuclear explosion occurs, a wave of intense electromagnetic energy is transmitted as a side effect, and this radiation burns out the delicate silicon chips and transistors found in modern electrical equipment, rendering hardware such as computers, radios and telephones useless. The phenomenon is known as EMP – or electromagnetic pulse effect.

When the United States tested out an atomic bomb in the 1960s, it was said to have blacked out a nearby city because of EMP. A military-funded study has discovered that the only intact transport vehicles that would work after a nuclear war would be primitive steam-driven trains, which have no delicate electrical components. It therefore seems entirely possible that the Strategic Reserve is indeed a reality, and that the old escapee from the nursing home had unwittingly stumbled upon one part of it.

THE SCOTLAND ROAD HOBGOBLIN

The following incredible story concerns a man who left Liverpool when he was fourteen to emigrate to Canada, where he settled in Montreal. The tale came my way by email from relatives of the person involved, and, due to the sensitive nature of the story, I have had to make a few minimal changes to names, but the events and places have not been altered.

In Canada in the mid-1950s, Sam, a sixty-year-old Liverpool-born man, began to have a series of distressing epileptic fits. The diagnosis looked grim – it was found that he had a brain tumour. Wilder Penfield, a brilliant sixty-four-year-old neurosurgeon, had decided to operate and began by carefully sawing off a section of Sam's skull-cap. Sam was wide awake during the operation – only local anaesthetic had been used. It is a little-known fact that, although the brain registers pain and sensation, it cannot itself feel pain. All the same, Sam could hear the circular blade of the electric saw whining away and could not only feel his head vibrating as it sliced through his skull, he could also smell burning bone.

Penfield, the greatest brain surgeon of his day, slowly and carefully explored Sam's brain, and as he did so, he chatted to his patient in a very reassuring tone, which was no mean feat, given the exceptional circumstances. He asked him about his occupation and Sam said that he was an insurance salesman. Penfield told him that he should not be alarmed if he felt any strange sensations, as it was perfectly normal – it was just the brain reacting to his exploratory survey. Sam found his eyes rolling a bit as Penfield touched one particular area of his brain with a tiny electrode. Then Sam lost control of his bladder, as Penfield touched another part of the brain. Penfield eventually located the tumour and a cancer specialist who was also present took a sample from it. The skullcap was replaced and Sam's head was bandaged up.

It turned out that the tumour was not cancerous; it was benign, but it would have to be removed, as it was causing dangerous pressure to build up inside the skull, causing the fits.

A week later, Penfield and another surgeon once again opened up Sam's head, and once again, Sam was only given a local anaesthetic. The tumour was removed without complications. In the course of the operation, Penfield told Sam about an amazing discovery: if a certain part of the brain's outer skin, or cortex, as it was called, was stimulated with a very low-powered current of electricity, it caused the patient to relive memories from long ago. Patients had reported being transported back to their childhood, to their teenaged years, and to certain minor incidents in their life they'd long forgotten. Wilder Penfield asked Sam if he could try out the technique on him, as he was carrying out research into human memory, and was in need of human guinea pigs to advance the understanding of the brain. Sam had a lot of faith in the surgeon and gave his permission.

Penfield carefully applied an electrode to a certain spot on the brain, and all of a sudden, Sam was transported back to his Liverpool home on Scotland Road. The year was 1905, and it was a beautiful spring day. Sam had a delicious lump of treacle toffee lodged in his mouth – it was so thick that he could hardly prise open his jaws. A tall policeman with a curled-up moustache walked past and smiled down at him, and horses and carts clattered along on the cobbled roads. Sam felt he was ten years of age, and his bodily senses told him he was actually there on Scottie Road. He passed all the familiar shops, and beheld all the well-known faces from his childhood.

Then Sam's heart somersaulted – here was the only woman he had truly loved with all of his heart; his Irish grandmother, Mary. She was coming out of the grocers with a covered basket, and Sam grabbed her hand and walked along with her. He wrenched his mouth open, despite the treacle toffee, and shouted, "Gran!"

"Watch yer don't choke tryin' to eat and talk at the same time," his grandma warned him.

Sam looked up and his gran's face, silhouetted against the blue sky of 1905, faded into a sterile white ceiling. He was back in the operating theatre.

The electrode was reapplied, and once again, Sam found himself instantly transported back to his childhood, only this time he beheld a terrible scene. His younger sister Maureen was sitting in the corner of a dark room, curled up and crying with her head between her knees. Sam kept asking her what was troubling her, but she couldn't speak because she was too upset. Sam then wandered out of the room and along the landing. He entered a bedroom, and there was his beloved Uncle Seamus. He was lying in a tiny bed, a bed that was comically too small. Seamus was dead, and he had a terrible expression on his face. His eyes were bulging in absolute terror.

Suddenly, there was a scream. Sam's grandmother threw herself on the bed, and frantically tried to wake up her dead son. Sam started to cry. Again, he returned to the present, and related the vivid memories to Penfield, who tape-recorded them. Sam was absolutely fascinated by the memories, and started to remember more things. He asked Penfield to continue his experiment, and the surgeon stimulated the same spot again.

This time Sam found himself in another nightmarish scene. He was lying on his bed, when young Maureen came in and said, "Sam, guess who's here?" Sam felt paralysed with fear, because he knew who it was. A green 'thing', some three feet in height, came into the room. It had pointed ears, large red eyes, and a wide, gaping mouth, rimmed with pointed teeth. This thing lived in an old well in the cellar of the house. His grandmother had told him it was a surviving hobgoblin.

As Sam stared, transfixed at the grotesque thing, it leapt like a cat on to him, and he was so utterly terrified that he passed out. He woke up in a cold sweat, and the surgeon had to calm him down. Undeterred, Sam asked Penfield to stimulate his memory cortex once again, but the surgeon said he had already carried out as many stimulations as was feasible, and he was not prepared to exceed the safety limit. The section of skull-cap was replaced, the scalp was re-stitched to the rest of the head, and Sam's cranium was carefully bandaged.

He was in hospital for a fortnight, and during that time, the loosened memories of his Scotland Road childhood came flooding back into his tampered-with mind. What Sam remembered left him angry and upset. He recalled seeing his Uncle Seamus holding Maureen on his knee. He recalled how the man tried to put his hand up his sister's dress, and how little Maureen pushed his hand back, again and again. Then he saw Maureen crying in the corner again. Seamus had done something very wrong to her.

Then, Sam remembered one particular night when Seamus had been climbing into the little bed where Maureen was sleeping. The girl shrieked and recoiled away from her tormentor, her face contorted with fear and loathing. That night help had come in an unusual form – the green hobgoblin from the cellar burst into the room, and making a hideous screeching sound as it grabbed Seamus by the throat, it shook him until he went limp.

Seamus died from the shock of being attacked by the demonic monstrosity. When Sam's grandmother found her son dead she said he had a weak heart. But Sam and Maureen knew better. Maureen had sworn Sam to secrecy and he promised never to tell anyone about her unsightly saviour.

After the incident, Sam had blotted out the memory of Seamus's vile behaviour. He'd repressed it in the way so many of us do when coping with a deeply traumatic event.

He recovered from his brain operation and later plucked up the courage to telephone Maureen, who was then living in London, and told her about the unsettling memories which had been brought to the surface by the operation. She confirmed every detail of them. Over the years she had convinced herself that she had imagined the hobgoblin in her old home at Scotland Place.

Maureen then did her own research and discovered that in Victorian times there was a legend of a mysterious creature which occasionally emerged from an ancient well on Scotland Road. The creature was known as the Hobgoblin of Scotland Road by the superstitious Irish emigrants. For Maureen, the mysterious creature had resolved a problem which had been going on for many years and had robbed her of her childhood.

GAS LAMP GHOUL

The following story took place in the early 1970s at a house in the south-end of Liverpool. A man named Mike bought one of the grand old terraced houses on North Hill Street, and decided to modernise it. He began by demolishing two walls in the building to create a large, spacious lounge. He also had the ceiling removed and a new one put in much higher up. A huge cast iron fireplace was installed, and then, after the walls were plastered and the carpets laid, Mike's wife, Frances, thought an old authentic Victorian lamp-post situated in the corner would be a lovely finishing touch. Mike said it would take some trouble obtaining one and fitting it in place, but Frances was an expert sulker, and so he put out his feelers to see if he could acquire an old gas lamp-post.

At the local pub, two brothers offered to uproot a lamp-post from Canning Street, or Rodney Street, for four hundred pounds. Mike dismissed their proposition as a ridiculous and illegal idea, and so he decided to explore another avenue. He asked a local man, Mr Dewhurst, who had a scrap-yard in the Dingle, if he could obtain an old Victorian, or even Edwardian lamp-post, and Dewhurst said he could, as he had a friend in Bedworth, Warwickshire, who specialised in providing Victorian memorabilia, and he knew that this man had a number of old lamp-posts.

Within three days, a black, cast-iron pillar, surmounted by a huge square lantern, had arrived by lorry at the house on North Hill Street. It was brought indoors and expertly installed in the lounge, and an electrician wired up a suitable soft yellow light in the housing of the lamp-post's lantern. Delighted with her new possession, Mike's wife put a ladder against the crossbar at the top of the lamp-post and climbed up it to clean the four glass panes.

That night, the couple sat on their old leather chesterfield sipping a glass wine, and surveyed their new lounge with its old lamp-post taking pride of place.

"You'd do anything for me, wouldn't you, love?" Frances said to Mike as she snuggled into his arms.

Mike was about to reply when he heard a strange, unfamiliar, musical sound.

"What was that?" asked Frances.

The couple sat up on the sofa, but as they strained their ears to listen to the noise, the ornamental clock on the mantelpiece started to chime the hour of midnight.

As the twelfth chime faded, Mike and Frances once more heard the odd jumble of tones, and both agreed that it sounded like an old-fashioned street barrel-organ. The music seemed to drift right into the lounge, but just as quickly it diminished again. The couple decided – or hoped – that it had been nothing more than the music from the radio of a passing car. Mike reassured his wife that sound travelled further at night, and could play tricks on the ears.

Eventually they went to bed, and at two in the morning, their seventeen-year-old daughter, Carol, crept into the house, having just returned from a nightclub. She went straight to the fridge, then heard eerie music coming from the lounge. She turned around, and was confronted by a terrifying apparition of a young man in grey, old-fashioned clothes. On his head he wore a strange pointed white cap. His face was of a ghastly purple hue, and his eyes were bulging out of their sockets. The man's tongue was completely black and was hanging out of his mouth as if it had been wrenched out. That was disturbing enough, but what made it worse was the way his head was tilted sideways at an unnatural angle – as if his neck was broken. The part of the kitchen where the gruesome apparition stood seemed to be shrouded in shadow.

Carol threw a carton of milk at the apparition and ran screaming out of the kitchen and into the back yard, then dashed all the way to a friend's house. Carol's parents rushed from their beds upon hearing the screams and found the spilt milk all over the kitchen, and the door to the back yard wide open. They followed her to Carol's friend's and found their daughter in a dreadful state. When she told them about the ghastly man who had appeared in the house, they thought she had been given LSD by someone in the club and must have been hallucinating. They brought her home and calmed her down, and she eventually went to bed at around six o'clock that morning.

A few nights later, Frances was working late, and Mike was sitting in front of the fire, doing a crossword, when he heard a fizzing, hissing sound. He looked up, and saw a flickering yellow flame behind the glass panes of the lamp-post. Once again he heard the strange barrel-organ music, and this time he heard faint voices, cheering and laughing. As Mike rose from his chair in astonishment, the voiced ended abruptly, and the jet of flame became an electric bulb once more in the lamp-post.

Mike felt uneasy in the house on his own, so he went to pick up his wife from work. When he returned home forty minutes later, there was a police car outside the house, and a gaggle of neighbours crowding round his front door. It transpired that one of his neighbours had called at the house, and had peered through the blinds in the lounge, where they had seen a man hanging from the old lamp-post. His body was jerking and his legs were kicking about violently. The neighbour flagged down a policeman passing by in a patrol car. The policeman also saw the hanged man, so he immediately kicked down the door – but upon entering the lounge, found, to his consternation, that the man had vanished into thin air. The two men who had seen the hanging figure had both noticed the strange white pointed hat it wore.

Suspecting that the old lamp-post was haunted, a Catholic priest was called in to bless and exorcise the ghost, or whatever it had been, on the following afternoon. As the priest was blessing the lamp-post, an old tailor's cloth tape measure flew up from a chair and wound itself tightly around the priest's neck, almost throttling him. Having disentangled himself, the priest continued his blessing, and the organ music was briefly heard once more.

As soon as the priest had finished his work, Mike and Frances had that lamp-post removed from the house and gave it away to a scrap-dealer. He allegedly sold it to the City Council, and it was later used to replace an old lamp-post on Rodney Street.

Mike and Frances spent almost four years carrying out research to establish if anyone had ever been lynched on a lamp-post in the area from where they had obtained the gas lamp. They eventually discovered, through a local historian, that on 29 January 1876, a retarded young man was hanged from a lamp-post by a drunken mob down in Bedworth. As the youth was hanged, a barrel-organ played, and hot potatoes were even sold to the crowds of bloodthirsty spectators. Mike and Frances found an illustration of the lynching from an old edition of the *Illustrated Police News*. The hanged man wore a white pointed dunce cap, and the style of lamp-post in the drawing exactly matched the lamp-post Mike had purchased.

TRUE COLOURS

One day I was walking along Hope Street on my way to investigate an alleged ghost sighting, when I happened to see a gang of small children, happily engaged in a game of football near an alleyway on Blackburne Place. The children were of different races, and it made an endearing and poignant sight, as just a few feet from where they were playing, stood the house where a racist woman once lived, many years before in the 1930s.

Grace Askworth had been brought up to believe that the colour of a person's skin determined his or her station in life. Her father had instilled the notion into her mind that white people were superior, and so, by the time Grace reached the age of twenty-one, her prejudices were firmly set into her way of thinking. The political situation in Britain and other parts of Europe seemed to vindicate Grace's racial views. Hitler was making his steady rise to power in Germany as he sought to 'cleanse the fatherland' of Jews, gypsies, and other ethnic minorities. Here in England, in 1932, Sir Oswald Mosley founded the British Union of Fascists, which incited violence against black and Jewish people. Members of Mosley's party wore black shirts and gave the Hitler salute.

In 1935, the women of Mosley's Fascist party went on parade in Liverpool, and Grace Askworth was one of the young people who watched the procession of women dressed in black berets, black shirts, and white, calf-length skirts. Observing the parade with considerably less approval, on the other side of Blackburne Place, with a canvas bag slung across his shoulder, was a black merchant seaman of about thirty years of age named Danny.

Whenever he docked in Liverpool he was given lodgings by a family in the area, and had just returned from New York. In a week's time he was off on another voyage, this time to Sydney. Danny had been born in Jamaica, but at the age of six he had been brought to Liverpool by his aunt, after his parents had both died in a blazing building.

As the black-shirted women passed by, two men from the crowd who were cheering the march, spat at Danny. Danny had never shied away from trouble in his life, and was ready to retaliate, but soon found that the rest of the mob was also against him, so, deciding that discretion was the better part of valour, he wisely backed away and quickly made his way to the safety of his lodgings.

Across the road, Grace had been inspired by the march and had decided that she would join the Fascist movement. The next day she wrote to their headquarters in London, requesting membership. Her father backed her decision wholeheartedly.

On the following day, which was a Sunday, Grace took her six-year-old niece Jemima for a walk. Jemima had long, blonde, flaxen hair, and a perfect, almost doll-like face. She had been born blind, and her world was one of scents, sounds and touch: the sensation of sunshine on her face, the faint hum of a dragonfly, the sweet aromas of the flowers in the park, things most of us never notice.

Upon this summer afternoon, Jemima clutched her Aunt Grace's hand as she skipped along to the sweetshop on the corner of the street, when she heard the curious and comical sound of a man singing in a deep, resonant voice. The girl smiled, and Danny, the owner of the voice, said, "I see you smiling, miss."

The girl blushed, and Grace quickly pushed her into the shop.

"Come along now, Jemima. We don't talk to people like that," she said.

Danny also entered the shop and asked for tobacco, but was sharply told to wait until the lady had been served. Grace deliberately took her time, then finally ordered a bag of boiled sweets for Jemima. Danny again politely asked for the tobacco and was begrudgingly served by the shop assistant in a deliberately condescending manner.

"Good morning," said Danny, as he left the shop, but received no reply.

On the pavement outside, he came upon a most distressing scene. Jemima was choking on one of the boiled sweets. She clutched her throat and was making a dreadful gagging sound as her aunt thrust her fingers into the girl's tiny mouth, attempting to remove the sweet. She couldn't, and Jemima sank to her knees, desperately clutching at Grace's skirt.

"Somebody help!" Grace shouted. "Please, help!"

A man ran off to fetch a doctor and Danny took the choking girl in his arms, as Grace protested vehemently. Jemima's body felt like a lifeless sack. Taking charge of the situation, Danny put his arms around the girl's waist and gently moved his fist upwards, under her ribcage, and squeezed. The second time he did this, the sweet fell from her mouth. He then gently laid the girl down and revived her by carrying out mouth to mouth resuscitation. After a few agonising minutes, in which Grace scarcely dared breathe, Jemima regained consciousness.

By the time the doctor eventually arrived, Danny was gone, and Grace realised that, in the panic, she had forgotten to thank him. When Jemima later asked about the man who had saved her life, her grandfather told her that he had been a black man. Jemima said that he was very kind and then asked an innocent question: "Are you a black man, Grandfather?"

Her grandfather was incensed by the question. "No! I certainly am not," was his bad-tempered reply.

But the whole incident, and particularly Jemima's question, had made Grace Askworth realise how insignificant the colour of a person's skin really was. In the dark, or to a blind person, there are no different skin colours,

The next day a letter of reply came from the Fascist party and Grace immediately tore it up and threw it on the fire. A blind girl had opened her eyes.

WHO WAS SIR PETER ROBINSON?

In the early 1860s, a dashing, handsome, yet enigmatic dandy, burst on to the high-society Liverpool scene and created a mystery that remained unsolved for generations.

One wintry evening, Sir Peter Robinson stepped out of the fog-bound streets of Liverpool like some spectre without a past, and entered, uninvited into a soirée, where he captivated the guests and set many female pulses racing with his youthful good looks and athletic build. When questioned, he asserted that he was one Lord Loxley, and not a single person bothered to consult the pages of *Burke's Peerage* to check whether Sir Peter was indeed one of the nobility.

Within seven calendar months, Lord Loxley disappeared as mysteriously as he had first appeared. The fascination which the vanished nobleman left in his wake was as intense as the intrigue which surrounded the disappearance of Lord Lucan a hundred years later. For many years, people in the upper echelons of Liverpudlian society often wondered what had become of Sir Peter Robinson. Theories abounded. Was he a phantom? Perhaps the Devil in a top hat and coat tails? For even when he was regularly seen in the city, no one had ever discovered exactly where Sir Peter lived, or from whence he came. Was he some foreign spy? The illegitimate offspring of a royal? A polished charlatan? What follows is the truthful answer, which was divulged to me by a descendant of the 'Lord'.

In January 1862, sixteen-year-old Charlotte 'Lottie' Watkins, noticed a small card in the parlour window of a house on Duke Street which read:

Parlourmaid wanted – thoroughly able to clean silver plate, wait well, and have an ability for plain needlework. Good personal character and references essential. Apply within.

Lottie obtained references from a previous employer and returned to the house in her Sunday best. She was admitted by Mr Chivers, a very old and decrepit servant, and ushered into the sitting room, where a very frail and ill-looking woman, Mrs Ransom, interviewed her. The interview was successful and Lottie was subsequently hired.

Not long afterwards, a vacancy arose for a servant to replace Chivers, who was shortly due to retire, so Lottie suggested her nineteen-year-old brother, George Watkins, who held a boring and poorly paid job in a tobacconist's shop on Richmond Row. To Lottie's delight, George was hired.

George Watkins and his sister took over the care of Mrs Ransom, whose health deteriorated to such an extent that she ended up confined to bed. A doctor visited and told the servants that, since the death of her husband six months previously, Mrs Ransom had gone into a decline. The physician advised complete rest. This left George and Lottie the run of the Duke Street house, and the decrepit servant downstairs, Mr Chivers, rarely ventured up the long flights of stairs to visit his mistress, his health being almost as bad as hers.

One evening, George Watkins went missing, and Lottie eventually found him in a huge, second-floor room which the late Mr Ransom had used as his dressing-room. Lottie found George posing before a full-length mirror, dressed in a silken top hat, Inverness cape, and long chequered coat. Upon his left hand, which twirled a walking stick with an ornate silver handle, Lottie noticed an impressive ring, set with a large scarlet bloodstone. With a flourish, the cheeky teenager then applied a monacle to his left eye as the finishing touch. Georgie looked quite the dandy as he studied his reflection from every angle in the enormous mahogany mirror, and complimented himself, speaking to his reflection in a mock, high-class accent.

Lottie was totally shocked. "Take those clothes off at once, George. Just who do you think you are?"

"Why, I am Sir Peter Robinson, Lord Loxley, my dear!" Georgie replied in a passably well-spoken voice. He possessed an amazing talent for imitation, and had 'stolen' the voice from a well-to-do customer who had frequented the tobacconist's shop in Everton. Lottie couldn't suppress a giggle as her brother paraded about the room, having imaginary conversations with members of the gentry and even the Queen herself!

That should have been the end of the joke, but that night, the top-hatted Georgie Watkins departed the house on Duke Street and strolled through the foggy night in his borrowed finery. Policemen saluted him, and even the ladies of the night on Paradise Street propositioned him with the utmost respect. After some time walking the streets masquerading as Sir Peter Robinson, Georgie was returning to Duke Street, when an old vagrant approached him and asked if he could spare a few farthings.

"I cannot, sir," Georgie said, because he carried no money.

The tramp smiled knowingly, and said, "Someone high-falutin' like you with no money? Strikes me as strange, sir. Goodnight."

Taking care that he was not being observed, Georgie rushed round to the tradesman's entrance and sidled into the Duke Street house, where he changed his clothes in the room upstairs. It had been such a thrill to impersonate one of the élite, and he lay in bed that night going over the night's events in his mind and planning his next exploit.

Days later, a letter, from His Worship the Lord Mayor, inviting the widow Mrs Ransom, and a friend to a ball at the Town Hall, arrived at the house. Mrs Ransom was far too ill to contemplate such an outing, so Georgie decided that Sir Peter Robinson should attend the ball instead. He inspected the card which had accompanied the letter, and saw that it didn't name a particular person, so he went along to the ball full of confidence. Sir Peter Robinson was received by the Lord Mayor, and every woman, young and old, was fascinated by the mysterious young Lord. Georgie was an exceptionally good dancer, and everybody watched admiringly as he danced the polka and waltzed elegantly about the hall.

The champagne flowed, and Sir Peter became more and more outrageous. He brazenly carried a merchant's wife on to the balcony and kissed her passionately in front of her husband. Naturally, the infuriated husband protested vehemently, upon which Sir Peter challenged him to a duel, but the merchant backed off, grumbling about the nobility thinking they were above the law.

That night, as carriages left the Town Hall, to take the revellers home, everyone was talking about the charming, yet outrageous Sir Peter Robinson. Men, whilst publicly protesting about his shocking behaviour, secretly wished that they could be as audacious as him, and many women secretly desired him as a lover.

A special carriage was laid on for Sir Peter to carry him home to his Duke Street residence. He arrived home, so full of champagne that he could hardly keep on his feet, and once the carriage had trundled off, he staggered stealthily to the tradesman's entrance in the alleyway. Once more, Georgie came upon the perceptive old tramp lurking in the alley. Feeling generous because of the drink, he brought him into the kitchen, and they sat down and ate supper together. The tramp openly questioned George's ancestry, saying that he knew he was nothing more than a servant, but apparently he saw the funny side of the deception. He assured George that his secret was safe with him, and after the supper, the agreeable and grateful vagrant left. He was invited into the kitchen on several more occasions, and became a friend of both George and Lottie Watkins.

By July, Sir Peter Robinson was the talk of the town, and people vied to have him as a guest at their parties. On one occasion he was invited to a lavish ball at the Adelphi Hotel, where he met Mohammed Said, the Viceroy of Egypt, and the Lord Mayor, who was now on first name terms with 'Sir Peter'. At the same event there was a small round portly man with a large moustache which merged with his fashionable long side whiskers, or 'Piccadilly Weepers' as they were called. This man, who looked tantalisingly familiar to Georgie, was introduced to him as Mr Arthur Vincent, a retired judge and colonel who had been wounded at the Battle of Balaclava in the Crimean War. Georgie listened as Mr Vincent was talking about his blood-curdling exploits in the Crimea to a circle of fascinated men and women.

Later that night, Mr Vincent confronted George in a secluded corner and in a hushed tone said, "You, sir, are a fake!"

George bravely kept up the pretence, despite a sickening feeling in his stomach, and threatened to sue Mr Vincent for slander. The fat old raconteur was having none of it.

"You are no more a Lord than the man in the moon! You work in a tobacconist's shop on Richmond Row," he growled.

Georgie's heart missed a beat. Now he knew why Mr Vincent had looked so familiar. He used to serve him tobacco when he worked in the shop. In whispers, Mr Vincent interrogated the young impostor, and that night, after the party, he travelled to the Ransom household with George to make the necessary arrangements for blackmail. The stipulation was that Georgie would pay out several guineas each week to Mr Vincent, or the police would be informed about the very grave offence of impersonating a Lord. Arthur Vincent was sitting in the kitchen, smugly sipping a large brandy, when in walked Lottie with the old tramp. When Mr Vincent saw the tramp his jaw dropped, as if he recognised him. After a long silence, the tramp said, "Well, well! Look who it is! Mr Percy Lilly, or lily-livered Lilly as we called him."

Mr Vincent got to his feet and stumbled backwards in shock, knocking over a chair.

"How dare you, you impertinent fellow! What are you doing in a house such as this? Get out this minute, or I will call the constabulary."

"You're mistaken; his name isn't Lilly, it's Vincent," said George. "He's a retired judge."

"Yes, and I'm the Prince of Wales," said the tramp. "He's no retired judge, he's a deserter!"

A pallid Mr Vincent quickly turned and, without a word, left the kitchen visibly shaken. Perhaps it was the shock which Mr Vincent had suffered that night, or perhaps it was just natural causes, but days afterwards, he collapsed and later died at the Royal Infirmary, where his true identity was quickly established. The doctors found a blue letter 'D' tattooed on his arm – the mark of a deserter – inscribed there by an army doctor. The man's name had indeed been Percy Lilly.

Suddenly, Georgie's recent fun and games lost its appeal – he had learned his lesson. He carefully replaced all of the late Mr Ransom's finery back in his dressing-room and never dressed up as a Lord again. But for years afterwards, at upper class parties and gatherings, many guests would speculate as to what had become of that dashing young bachelor, Sir Peter Robinson.

THE BOOK OF PROVERBS

In December 2000, John Reece, a fifty-five-year-old Aigburth businessman, was casually perusing through various old-fashioned tomes in a certain antiquarian bookshop in the north west, when he happened to come upon a beautiful, wine-coloured, leather-bound Victorian diary for the year 1889. There were no entries or notes written within the diary; it had never been used. On some of the dates, the diary gave information about sunrise, sunset, the phases of the moon, the feast days of the saints, which date Ash Wednesday fell upon and so forth. Also, on certain dates, there were proverbs and sayings printed in italics; a sort of 'thought for the day'.

Mr Reece purchased the diary for three pounds and took it home. On New Year's Day 2002, he realised that the diary of 1889 corresponded exactly with the days and dates of the year 2002, so he decided to use it for the year ahead. He jotted down the days when he would be off work during January, and as he turned to the page for the 17 and 18 of that month, he noticed that there were a couple of proverbs corresponding to those two days. The first one morbidly stated: 'Death surprises us in the midst of our hopes.' The second one read: 'The course of true love never did run smooth.'

On the first of those two dates, Harry, a close friend of Reece's, literally dropped dead in the parlour of his pub. Ironically, Harry had just been telling John Reece that he had been to the doctor, and that his usually high blood pressure was now back to a normal level, and he had also been carefully watching his diet. Just a few seconds after he had told Mr Reece this, he had collapsed from heart failure and landed at his friend's feet. John Reece later thought about the proverb for that day in the diary, and recalled how it had said: 'Death surprises us in the midst of our hopes'.

"Must have been a coincidence," he thought, despite a feeling of slight uneasiness.

On the following day, Mr Reece bumped into an old flame named Barbara, and he persuaded her to go to a wine bar on Lark Lane with him, where they ended up reminiscing about old times. Several glasses of wine later, John and Barbara were intimately holding hands and thoroughly enjoying each other's company. Barbara went home with him, but that night, John said something to upset her. He made some flippant remark without thinking first, and Barbara slapped his face and then left. John Reece later looked at the old diary for that date, and re-read the quotation which aptly said, 'The course of true love never did run smooth'. That had to be a coincidence as well – surely?

With thoughts of trying to win back Barbara weighing heavily on his mind, Reece flipped the pages of the diary and they fell open on Thursday 14 February – Valentine's Day. The proverb for the one date in the calendar associated with love was appropriately printed in red, and it declared: 'Opportunity seldom knocks twice'.

This set John wondering. Was the proverb a warning to grasp the moment and the seize the chance to ask Barbara to be his wife? He decided that it may well have some significance and resolved to propose to her on that date, rather than perhaps miss the opportunity forever.

On Valentine's Day then, Reece made arrangements to take Barbara to a top class restaurant. He meticulously prepared for the evening: spending ages in the bathroom, dressing in his most expensive suit and finally splashing on a generous dose of aftershave. He looked anxiously again at the engagement ring he'd purchased from Boodle and Dunthorne – a blue sapphire set in platinum, which had cost him two thousand pounds. As he was getting ready to leave for Barbara's home, his telephone started to ring, but, not wanting to be late, he quickly switched on his answering machine and from it, he heard the distinctive voice of his friend Mike, who lived down in Wrexham.

A hackney cab sounded it's horn outside.

"Sorry, Mike," John said to himself as he anxiously glanced at his watch. He left the house in a hurry, purposely turning off his mobile as he entered the taxi. Nothing was going to be allowed to interrupt tonight's plans, which he hoped would mark the end of his bachelor lifestyle.

At the restaurant, Barbara seemed to be acting strangely. She appeared distant, as if she had something weighing heavily on her mind. Towards the end of the meal, which John thought had gone very well, he plucked up courage and said, "Barbara, I want to ask you a very important question, and I think you know what the question is going to be." He took the small velvet box from his pocket and placed it on the tablecloth in front of her. She said nothing and her eyes closed for a while, and when they opened, tears streamed from them. John surmised that she was crying because she was so overcome by the impending proposal of marriage.

However, when she did start to speak, Barbara said she had only come on the Valentine date to tell him something important. She had met a man several months ago, and intended to marry him. She would have been spending Valentine's Day with him, but he was working down in London. She had thought it would be fitting to use the date to let John know that he was still a friend, and a very good one at that, but she felt no love for him anymore, and hoped he would understand. If she had known he had intended to propose, she would never have come to the restaurant.

John was devastated, and in a choked voice, said, "You decided to tell me on this day of all days? I'll never understand the mind of a woman."

Barbara started to sob, and quickly left, saying she was sorry.

When John Reece got home he listened to the messages on his telephone answering machine. His friend from Wrexham said he urgently needed twenty thousand pounds to put into a business opportunity that had arisen unexpectedly. A bistro with amazing prospects had come on the market, and Mike just needed twenty thousand pounds to seal a business arrangement which would make him the owner of the bistro, which was located in a popular area of Dublin. Mike called back four times that evening, and on the fourth call he told John that the money had now been put up by another friend. That bistro is now flourishing, and Mike is set to open up another one in Ireland. John Reece quickly realised that, once again, the old diary had seemingly forewarned him about his lost chance with the proverb, 'Opportunity seldom knocks twice'.

From that time onwards, John Reece became obsessed with the diary and its proverbs. He flipped through the pages, reading each of the sinister proverbs – and one in particular, for July, made his blood run cold. Its stark message read, 'The best go first'. What could this mean? Would he lose someone close to him on that date?

Sure enough, when the date arrived, John Reece heard that his best friend, who had emigrated to Australia many years before, had been knocked down and killed by a car near his home in Sydney.

It could all be dark coincidence, or perhaps that diary of long ago really *did* have the power to foretell the future.

LIFE STORY

I first heard about this unusual tale many years ago, and several people who personally knew the man who is the subject of the story have backed it up with their own accounts of the strange incident.

Around 1958, forty-five-year-old Tommy MacIntyre went to visit his seven-year-old daughter Susan in the Children's Hospital in Myrtle Street, where she was due to have her adenoids removed. Tommy was separated from his wife. He was a drunkard, and a bully, who had left her black and blue on more than one occasion. So finally she had left him and taken their daughter with her to a house in Devonshire Road, in Toxteth.

Anyway, on this night he told his little girl she'd be fine, and he hugged and kissed her, and then left the hospital – and walked straight into a local pub called The Mulberry Bush. There he downed three pints, then went on to the Red House pub on the corner of Crown Street, where he knocked back several shots of rum in quick succession. As was usual, he became rather bellicose in drink, and after threatening a fellow drinker at the Red House, the landlord ejected him from the premises.

Tommy McIntyre then turned up at the Bear's Paw in Paddington, where he was involved in yet another altercation. From there he staggered to the Weighing Machine pub on Wavertree Road, where he threatened to throw a bar stool through a jukebox, because the music being played on the premises wasn't to his liking. Once again he was thrown out of the pub. Within half an hour, McIntyre was causing a disturbance at the Leigh Arms, but even after two men roughly escorted him outside and threw him on to the pavement, he was still hungry for trouble.

Minutes later, on the Wavertree High Street, McIntyre made the mistake of calling two well-built Teddy Boys "big girls' blouses", because of their outlandish attire. They gave him a right pasting and left him bleeding and bruised on Pye Street. With a bloodied nose, a black eye and a ripped jacket, Tommy crawled down an alleyway which came out on Prince Alfred Road, and took refuge in what looked like a music hall. There was no one in the small foyer, so he walked into the dark auditorium unchallenged, and flopped down on a comfortable seat, nursing his badly bruised limbs. There was not one other soul about – all the seats were empty.

The lights suddenly dimmed, and a projector made a whirring sound somewhere behind him. A powerful beam of light cut through the air and a film was projected on to the silver screen. Even in his drunken, battered state, Tommy realised that he must have wandered into a cinema, albeit a very strange one. A silent film with no titles or credits commenced. The first scene showed a vaguely familiar building. Why did it seem so familiar to Tommy? Then he realised that it was the very same infant's school he had attended long ago. "What a coincidence," he thought.

Then his heart jumped. Crowds of children started pouring into the street, and filing through the arched entrance into the school. Their mothers accompanied them. One boy and his mother remained at the entrance, and the film showed a close-up of the boy. He was crying, and his mother was wiping his tears away and smiling. He didn't want to go to school. That boy was Tommy MacIntyre! "Eh! What's going on? This's got to be a dream," Tommy thought, and his brain, addled with so much alcohol, sluggishly tried to fathom it out. If it was a dream, Tommy, filled with nostalgia, hoped he wouldn't wake up for a while. Tears streamed down his face as he watched his concerned and loving mother trying to get her son to let go of her hand on his first day at school.

The film continued, and breathtaking scenes of forgotten memories, long-dead friends, and long-demolished places were displayed before him in vivid monochrome. There was his old mongrel dog 'Blacky' that he had thought would live forever, running alongside him, always loyal. The drunkard watched as a young Tommy Mac turned the dog's ears inside out, and the Tommy of 1958 wiped away the tears and laughed as the dog violently shook its head.

Then followed another scene that had long been lost to memory. A scene which broke his heart. It was the moment when he found his grandmother lying dead in her armchair. He watched the nine-year-old Tommy shaking her, trying to wake her up. She looked as if she was asleep. Suddenly, the hurt in Tommy's heart made the aches and pains of the beating he had just received seem insignificant. On the screen, the young Tommy lay across his beloved grandmother, sobbing silently as Blacky tilted his head – his questioning, brown eyes looking puzzled and sorrowful.

Then came another scene that tore the inebriate's heart apart. His first love, at the tender age of thirteen, was Kate, who drifted into his life in the summer of 1926. They had planned to run away together, but she ended up falling for another boy. Tommy felt the sadness welling up in his throat and chest as he watched the pretty girl on the screen. All of the key moments, all of the golden memories of his life were shown, and, besides seeing the death of his grandmother, the ones that jolted his heart most were the scenes where he saw his wife's face for the first time, and the close-ups of the birth of his daughter. His emotions were in turmoil and he started to cry. He called out, "Stop it! Stop it! I don't want to see any more, I can't stand it!"

The invisible projectionist paid no heed to his cries. The film continued. It showed graphic scenes of McIntyre beating his wife in a drunken rage; little three-year-old Susan running into her bedroom and hiding under the

78

blankets; close-ups of the blood on his wife's face, her tears in close-up. It also showed all of the friends whom Tommy had driven away because of the constant drunken arguments and fights.

Then came the terrifying scene depicting the end result of all the drinking – a funeral. He saw the wake, with his own bloodless corpse wrapped in a white shroud in the coffin. His little girl, dressed in black, crying …

At this point, the film ended as mysteriously as it had begun. The whirring of the projector died down until a deathly hush descended on the deserted auditorium. Tommy MacIntyre rushed out of the cinema and made his way to his brother's house in a highly emotional state. He babbled out a fragmented, garbled account of the eerie film show of his own life – and death. His brother Alfie told him to calm down, and after listening to Tommy's incredible and spooky story, he reassured him that the 'film' was probably a product of the DTs. "There's no cinema on that road," Alfie confidently told his brother, but Tommy insisted that he had definitely been in a cinema on that road, DTs or no DTs.

Realising that things had reached crisis point, Alfie decided that he would have to help his brother, or he was doomed. With his support, Tommy became a changed man. The transformation didn't happen overnight, of course, and it certainly wasn't easy, but he did improve himself sufficiently to renew his wedding vows and turn himself into a decent husband and father about a year later.

Minutes after I broadcast an account of this strange story on the *Billy Butler Show*, several older listeners telephoned me to say that there had indeed been a cinema on Prince Alfred Road in the early days when every film was in black and white, but it had been demolished around 1950. This cinema was called The Magnet, and it stood next to the Prince Alfred pub. The cinema had therefore once stood on the exact same spot where Tommy McIntyre, a violent drunkard, ready for oblivion, was shown the story of his life and given a stark warning of what lay ahead for him unless he was able to rid himself of his ruinous addiction.

A Bridge Too Far

On the Friday night of 20 September 2001, forty-nine-year-old Tony left his home in Speke and drove in his transit van to his mother's house in the Windmill Hill area of Runcorn. Tony was due to spend Saturday and Sunday at his mother's home to help out with some decorating.

On Sunday, at around seven in the evening, Tony had to drive up to Halton Road to his cousin's house, to borrow a ladder to complete the rest of the decorating job. He realised that there was more work to do than he had initially estimated as he loaded his cousin's ladder, plus a few pots of exterior paint, into the transit van. He then began to drive back to his mother's at about 8.15pm.

Fifteen minutes into the journey, Tony received a frantic call on his mobile from his thirteen-year-old daughter Christina, who said that her mum had started being violently sick and was doubled up with stomach pains. Christina had already called for an ambulance. He called his mother and told her what had happened. She naturally agreed with him that he should return home immediately. At this point, Tony was situated somewhere near Boston Avenue, and it was here that events take a very strange turn.

In, extreme situations, lots of us do stupid things. We push at doors that say 'Pull' on them and can even forget our own names, addresses and telephone numbers. In Tony's case, it was dark, and he was never too familiar with the Runcorn area at the best of times. So it was no surprise that he lost his bearings after getting caught up in a succession of slow moving traffic queues and made the mistake which many motorists make: he decided to try a short cut, and ended up going in completely the wrong direction. Getting more and more desperate, he swore at the traffic signs beyond the windscreen, and decided to try another route. This decision brought him face-to-face with something which will baffle him for many years to come.

He came upon a modern, enormously long, unfamiliar bridge, which seemed to be located about half a mile east of Runcorn Bridge. This bridge was very obviously not Runcorn Bridge – it didn't have the distinctive arched hump for a start – it was straight and very long, probably about one and a half miles in total. The strangest thing of all was that there was not another single vehicle on this new bridge, which consisted of two dual carriageways going in opposite directions. Tony cagily drove on to the bridge, and fervently hoped that it wasn't still under construction, but by this time he was so beside himself that he didn't think about that too much. At one point he looked down from the bridge and saw a canal of some sort – perhaps the Manchester Ship Canal.

When Tony left the bridge, he found himself on a stretch of motorway that eventually led him on to another road network. At this point, he stopped to ask a motorist for directions, and when he told the driver he had taken the wrong bridge, he received a blank stare. There was only one bridge across the Mersey, the motorist told him.

Eventually, Tony reached Speke, where he stopped to call Christina. She didn't answer but a neighbour did, and she told him that Christina and her mother were in the hospital, where his wife was being operated on for acute appendicitis.

His wife later made a full recovery, at which point a very relieved Tony began thinking again about the night she was admitted to hospital, and particularly about the mysterious bridge. He soon returned to the area to try and satisfy himself that, despite all evidence to contrary, such a bridge actually existed, only to find that there was no such bridge.

Completely bewildered by the whole affair, he contacted me and I told him that in the year 2000 I had received a call from a Halton woman who had also seen a ghostly bridge spanning the Mersey at that point, which she estimated to be about a mile east of the original Runcorn Bridge. Perhaps the spectral bridge is some glimpse of a future bridge that is often talked about, but which has yet to be built.

In December 2000, the *Daily Post* reported that Halton Borough Council had appointed Chester-based engineering consultants, Gifford, to carry out feasibility studies for a new bridge across the River Mersey. An artist's impression of the new one hundred and fifty million pound bridge in the *Daily Post*, pictured the crossing situated half a mile east of the current Runcorn/Widnes bridge, and what's more, the bridge was straight and flat, without the distinctive hump of the present day bridge. It is hoped that the new bridge will solve congestion problems on the so-called 'Runcorn Expressway' bridge.

BLACK MARY

Over the years I have heard many ghost stories about the restless phantom of 'Black Mary', a shadowy apparition of a woman who roams St George's Hall. From my own researches, and from several reliable accounts about the spectre from people working at St George's Hall, I have managed to piece together the following:

Around 1989, in a window in a Bold Street shop that sold fine art, I once saw a beautiful oil painting by an obscure Lancashire artist from the Victorian period, William Osbert. Set in what was said to be Sefton Park, the subject of the painting was a palm reader who looked like the archetypal female gypsy of popular imagination, complete with the colourful headscarf and large gold loop earrings. Her face was dark, her green eyes large and mysterious, and surrounding the Romany mystic was a circle of well-to-do bonneted ladies carrying parasols. One of these upper class women was having her palm read by the gypsy woman. The title of the work was 'Palm-reading Sunday'. It was dated 1873, the year after the park had been officially opened by Prince Arthur. I inquired about the background to the painting, but the man in the art shop could tell me nothing beyond the fact that the work had been discovered several years previously at the house of a reclusive old woman on Charles Berrington Road in Wavertree.

One day I was gazing at the painting in the window, when an old man stopped beside me and peered at the same work of art. He complained that the sun would fade the painting, and that it ought to be placed in the shady interior of the shop. I agreed, and the man started to reel off some amazing tales about the painting. He told me that the palmist in the scene was a Hungarian woman named Mary Strang. She had been paid a guinea by William Osbert to pose for the portrait. This is the rest of what the old man told me that afternoon on Bold Street:

Mary Strang's predictions were so accurate and uncanny, that the Church and the authorities soon banned her from reading fortunes in Sefton Park, where, in the summer, she would read the delicate palms of ladies out on their Sunday strolls. Mary was very swarthy, with long black hair, and her beautiful green eyes were deep and penetrating. The gypsy had the reputation of being able to see into people's minds, and many avoided her because she could read their darkest desires and innermost secrets.

In the early 1890s, Mary upset a certain affluent Liverpool family by claiming that they were all cursed and would die terrible deaths because their ancestors had driven the poor people of Ireland out of their homes to die of starvation. Strangely enough, within a very short time, each member of the high class family that Mary had warned, started to die, one by one. The youngest died from scarlet fever, then his mother died soon after in a riding accident. The deaths continued until only the daughter was left, and she was placed in the care of relatives.

Black Mary, as Mary Strang was known, went on to make a very controversial accusation which ruffled the feathers of high class society. This took place one day, on St George's Plateau in Lime Street, where Mary was selling artificial flowers, when she noticed a well dressed gentleman approaching the entrance to St George's Hall. Mary offered him an imitation carnation, and the man allegedly struck out with his walking cane and rapped Mary's hand quite sharply. Mary yelled out in pain, then, closing her eyes and concentrating very hard, accused the man of committing several serious and illegal sexual offences. The man, who happened to be Sir Leslie Stephen (brother of the celebrated Judge Stephen, who had sentenced Florence Maybrick to death at St George's Hall) turned purple with rage. Sir Leslie immediately fetched a policeman and had Mary thrown into the cells under St George's Hall, without a hearing, or even an official arrest, to teach her a lesson.

There may have been some truth in Mary Strang's accusations, because Sir Leslie Stephen should have reported the woman for defamation of character and slander, but he decided instead to use his connections at St George's Hall, and had her put in one of the darkest, coldest cells in the bowels of the hall. Sir Leslie probably only intended to confine the gypsy for a few days, but the woman became seriously ill, and died soon afterwards, but not before she uttered a chilling curse.

Judge Stephen and his younger brother heard through the grapevine that the gypsy had put a curse of death upon Judge Stephen. She had also claimed that Sir Leslie would be plagued by illness until his death. Shortly afterwards, and for the rest of his life, Sir Leslie began to complain of dizzy spells, which left him nauseous, but no doctor, even the most eminent in Harley Street, could diagnose the cause of his perplexing symptoms.

Weeks after Mary Strang cursed Judge Stephen, he died a slow agonising death, with a look of absolute terror on his face. For hours on his deathbed he had been rambling on about the accursed Mary Strang, so many believed that the gypsy woman's deadly curse had truly come to pass.

Days after Black Mary's death, her ghost was seen roaming the cells of St George's Hall, and she even put in an appearance in the law courts. Many people who have worked at St George's Hall assure me that Mary's shade continues to haunt the place from time to time.

THE RETURN OF WALTER SLIM

A former student of the University of Liverpool rang me one afternoon at the studios of Radio Merseyside to relate a story I had heard something of before. I often hear several versions of an alleged supernatural event, and more often than not, I have to try and 'iron out' the inconsistencies of the varying accounts to avoid contradictions arising. The following story, however, was related to me over a period of almost three years, from no fewer than seven people, and all of their recollections regarding a very strange tale concurred entirely. The last piece of the jigsaw which made the story complete was the discovery of a name in a Liverpool cemetery which I happened to stumble upon. Without further ado, here is the eerie tale of Walter Slim.

On the evening of Friday 13 August 1971, at around nine o'clock, five male students left their lodgings on Liverpool's Upper Stanhope Street and headed for the Philharmonic pub on Hope Street. This was the so-called 'glam rock' era, with bands like T Rex appearing in the pop charts, and it wasn't unusual for the youth of the early seventies, especially students, to dress outlandishly. Two of the five students wore battered old top hats and Army trench-coats, and one even wore a deerstalker which sported a scarlet carnation. Fashion-wise, it was an era of anything goes.

The strangely-clad students decided to take a short cut through St James's cemetery next to the Anglican Cathedral, which is a creepy place even in broad daylight, but this was nine o'clock at night, and twilight heightened the supernatural menace of the vast graveyard. The students were glad when they had emerged unscathed on the other side of the cemetery, and they hurried past the Liverpool Institute (which is now the Fame School, LIPA).

At this point, one of the students, Douggie, noticed a stranger walking alongside them, wearing a top hat and a long black opera cloak. He also wore a white starched collar and a large bow tie. He was about six feet in height, and looked about thirty years old. His face was extremely pallid and anaemic-looking. Douggie nudged one of his friends, grimaced and asked, "Who's he?"

His friend looked at the stranger and shrugged. The students crossed Hardman Street, but the stranger stood rooted to the kerb, gazing in fascination at the cars waiting at the traffic lights. Douggie and his friends went into the spacious lounge of the Philharmonic pub, which was packed on this Friday night. Then, as Douggie was ordering a drink, he saw the top-hatted man in the cloak dash into the pub, throw back his cloak and screech with laughter. He looked as if he was demented, or possibly high on drugs. Everyone in the pub noticed the stranger and they all agreed that he was decidedly creepy. The barman looked him up and down and asked him what he wanted to drink, and in a strange-sounding voice the man said: "In the name of human charity, I'll have your gin, sir!"

The barman enquired how he wanted the gin, and the man in the topper impatiently waved his hand and shouted, "Gin, sir! Nothing else!" and he slapped the counter three times with the palm of his hand. Everyone backed off, because there was something extremely sinister about the man. A lot of people later recalled how he had given off an awful body odour, mingled with a sickly sweet scent, reminiscent of violets. The glass of gin was duly poured and placed before the eccentric stranger, and the barman held out his hand, expecting to be paid, but the stranger ignored him, swigging down the neat, undiluted gin and banging the glass down on the counter.

He then turned around and walked to a corner where a black girl was standing on her own. The girl was exceptionally beautiful and wore her hair in the popular 'Afro' style. She backed up against the wall as the malodorous man approached. He grabbed her hand, kissed her knuckle, and simultaneously tilted his hat. "My name is Walter Slim," he said, and his dark eyes seemed to smile, though his lips did not move. He asked the girl her name.

"Sarah," she said, very self-consciously.

"What a delightful name!" Walter chimed, and began to ramble on about how his father had supported the campaign to end the despicable institution of slavery. He then lapsed into sentimentality, and in a choked-up voice, he said, "Many, many years ago, I loved a girl named Sarah. The beautiful Miss Sarah Beaton."

Walter then produced a beautiful silver locket and opened it to show Sarah the oval portrait within of a young golden-haired lady. Tears rolled down Walter's face as he described how Sarah had died from a fever, just days before he was due to marry her. She had been just seventeen. The twentieth century Sarah felt great sympathy for the smelly stranger, and subconsciously realised that he must be some sort of flesh and blood ghost. For some reason she was no longer afraid.

"I feel quite ill," Walter said suddenly.

At this point, the barman who had been diddled out of his money, told him to get out, saying that he was permanently barred. Walter stumbled out of the pub into the night, with Sarah following him. Her friends begged her not to go after him, because he was obviously mad, but she ignored them and set off after him. She followed him to the cemetery nestling in the shadow of the Gothic splendour of the massive sandstone Anglican Cathedral, and she immediately noticed how he seemed terrified of the traffic plying its way along Rodney Street. Sarah squinted into the darkness and watched him stagger into the blackness until he could no longer be seen. She was afraid of the dark at the best of times and wisely decided against going into the cemetery alone.

Well, that should have been that. The incident went down in Liverpool folklore; the far-fetched tale of Walter Slim, the Victorian ghost who called in for a gin at the Philharmonic pub, had even reached my young ears when I was a child living off nearby Myrtle Street. Some thought the visitation was a hoax, staged by some madcap student with a dark sense of humour on that Friday the thirteenth.

Then, one evening in July 2002, I was in the Everyman Bistro when I happened to meet a man named Ken, who had once been a photographer for the *Liverpool Echo* many years before. We chatted on the subject of the paranormal, and Ken mentioned that he had once been called out to take a photograph of a huge, eight-pointed, occult symbol, which black magicians had drawn in the cellar of the derelict John Bagot Hospital in the north of the city. The dabblers in the Black Arts had drawn up the symbol in the old hospital, because so many people had died there over the years, and the occultists probably wanted to try and channel the energy that had been released at that location to open up a portal to demonic entities.

Ken later produced the actual photograph. I had seen the strange symbols in the photograph somewhere before. I checked them against a photograph I had in my possession of an identical eight-pointed star scrawled in the desecrated tomb of a Victorian gentleman in the Cathedral cemetery off Hope Street in 1971. When I checked the name on this tomb, I saw that it read: 'Walter Slim, 1861-1888'. He had died at the tender age of twenty-seven. I then remembered the old tale about the ghost walking into the Philharmonic pub. The other name mentioned had been a Sarah Beaton. I also located her grave in the same cemetery. She had died in 1885, aged seventeen.

The occultists who had broken into Walter Slim's tomb had carried out one of the most controversial and terrifying rituals in black magic, the 'Octagenesis of Resurrection', which is purported to be a way of raising the dead. However, the revived corpse usually disintegrates after an hour or so. Only perfectly preserved corpses, taken from a lead-lined coffin, are used in the ritual. Walter Slim was laid to rest in just such a lead coffin.

HAVEN'T WE MET SOMEWHERE BEFORE?

In October 1995, Janet, a twenty-five-year-old St Helen's woman, broke up with her boyfriend after she discovered he had been having an affair. The break-up of the relationship left Janet feeling very low, and so her friends decided to do something to get her back to her normal chirpy self. Late one evening, Janet and her two friends were listening to a lonely hearts radio programme called *Evening Encounter,* which involved listeners writing in to the radio presenter Pete Price with their personal details, the type of man or woman they were looking for etc. The listeners who liked the sound of what they heard would write in and a meeting would be arranged with an eye to romance.

On this particular night, the presenter read out a touching letter which he told the listeners came from a girl called Janet, who was twenty-five, and lived in the St Helen's area. Having just broken up with her boyfriend, she wanted to meet a considerate and loving man in the Merseyside area who would take her out, and would also spend cosy nights in with her. Janet's heart skipped a beat when she heard the letter being read out, because she realised it was referring to herself, and that it had been written by her two giggling friends whose voices she immediately recognised, and who had obviously decided to play Cupid.

There response to the letter was good. About five days later, twenty-two letters arrived at the radio station, and were passed on to Janet. In a fit of giggles, she and her friends read through them, and they all agreed that the most promising one was from thirty-two-year-old Murray, from Knowsley. He had enclosed a passport-type photograph in his letter, and seemed quite handsome. Janet thought the photograph looked strangely familiar, as if she knew Murray. She was convinced that she had seen him some place before.

Janet telephoned Murray, and the couple spent ages talking before arranging to meet in person at a pub in St Helens. Janet felt very peculiar when they met. She had a strong feeling of déjà vu, as if she had met Murray before somewhere, and the strange thing was, that Murray later said that he also felt as if they had met before, but he couldn't say where.

The couple walked across the lounge bar of the pub, and Murray pointed to two vacant chairs at a table near a blazing log fire, but, with considerable embarrassment, Janet told him she couldn't sit there, as she had suffered from a fear of fire all her life. Murray was very understanding, and sat in the corner and told Janet that he had a psychological hang-up over fire as well, only it wasn't a phobia – it was a mania. When he was a child, he had developed pyromania – a fixation with burning things. A lot of boys have this common fixation at that age, but Murray was put under a child psychiatrist because, at the age of seven, he had gathered together all his sister's dolls and had then burned them in a heap in the back yard. Even more alarmingly, he had also set fire to a girl's hair at school. He laughed off these incidents from his childhood, but all the talk of fire made Janet shudder.

Despite having such opposing hang-ups on the same subject, the couple continued to see one another, and a few days later, they went to a Halloween party. Janet dressed as a witch, complete with pointed hat and a long black Gothic dress. On seeing her outfit, Murray recoiled and his usually sociable personality underwent a drastic change.

"You shouldn't have dressed like that," he said ominously.

"Why, what's the matter with it?" Janet asked. "It's only a bit of fun."

"I can't stand witches, that's all. They just make my stomach churn. They're evil. They should stop all of this Halloween nonsense, it goes against God."

"For goodness sake, Murray, lighten up. It's a fancy dress party," said Janet. "I thought my outfit was spot on." And she leaned over to kiss him, but he seemed cold and distant all of a sudden.

Days later, Murray was driving Janet to another party. It was bonfire night, and as the car passed a field where a bonfire was blazing, Janet covered her face with her hands, because she was terrified of the way the crackling flames flickered across the children's faces, as they jeered at the smouldering Guy. Murray, meanwhile, slowed down the car and wound down the window to get a better view of the impressive bonfire. With eyes wide, he revelled at the wonderful odours of charred wood, and marvelled at how clean the flames seemed – how they seemed to sterilise, then devour, whatever they touched. Janet yelled for him to drive on, and eventually Murray reluctantly did so.

At the party, Janet and Murray were introduced to a man who was training to be a hypnotherapist. He claimed that he could remove any phobia through hypnotic regression. He would put a person in a trance using hypnosis, then dredge through their subconscious to find the root cause of the phobia.

He hypnotised Janet, and asked her why she hated fires so much. Under hypnosis she vividly remembered being an old woman – who was burned to death! She remembered her head being shaved, and a man pouring something inflammable on her scalp and back and then setting it alight. He put her in a large barrel, she said, and the brushwood around the barrel was also lit with a torch. She was a witch named Janet, being burnt alive. All about her, Janet could see all the laughing, jeering faces, distorted by the flames and intense, shimmering heat. One of those faces was very familiar – it was Murray! He held the flaming torch. At that point, Janet passed out from the agony of the searing flames – and found herself in total darkness and absolute silence.

The startled hypnotherapist quickly lifted the trance and Janet was carried to a sofa, where she gradually recovered from the painful, but illuminating, ordeal. The hypnotherapist later suggested hypnotising Murray, to see if he had actually been some sort of witchfinder in a previous life, but Murray sternly declined the offer, saying hypnotism was the work of the Devil.

About a year later, Murray and Janet were touring in Scotland on holiday, when they passed through a place called Dornoch. They both found that they somehow knew every part of this area, even though neither of them had ever been there before. Janet experienced an over-powering feeling that this was the place where she had been burnt at the stake in a previous life.

They decided to explore the place and Murray came upon a strange stone inscribed with the date 1727. Janet noticed a tourist taking photographs of the stone, and asked him what event the boulder marked. The tourist turned out to be very well informed and told them that a witch called Janet Horne had been burnt to death in a barrel of oil on that spot in 1727 – the last witch to be burned in Scotland. The account so closely matched Janet's experience under hypnosis, that she immediately felt faint, especially when she heard the name *Janet* Horne.

Janet later researched the witch-burning incident and discovered that Janet Horne had had her head shaved, and had then been doused with brandy. The flames would cleanse her soul before death, the witchfinders had announced. Murray later confessed that he had suffered vivid nightmares of flames burning Janet, but in the dreams, Janet had been much older.

Not surprisingly, the couple later split up, because they believed that in some previous existence, they had been murderer and victim.

JIGSAW JINX

The following strange story was related to me by a Mrs Bryant, an elderly listener to my radio programme. The tale has been told in the family for generations, and concerns Mrs Bryant's grandfather, George Ratcliffe, and his two younger brothers, Arthur and Eddie. Mrs Bryant asked me to research the tale, and I have established that something very strange did indeed take place concerning her grandfather and his brothers almost a hundred years ago.

In 1908, the three brothers lived in a small street off Heyworth Street in Everton. They were George Ratcliffe, aged twenty-one, Arthur Ratcliffe, aged sixteen, and fourteen-year-old Eddie. They lived with their mother and their father, who was wheelchair-bound due to a degenerative disease of the spine.

One summer morning in July 1908, the two younger Ratcliffe brothers received a shilling each – a fortune for a child in those days – from a visiting aunt, and they set off for a magnificent toyshop in Victoria Street to buy a few novelties. Children grew up much more slowly in those days and played with toys for far longer than today's computer generation. Young Edward bought a spinning top and whip, and a wind-up bird that flapped its feathered balsa wings and actually flew a short distance, and he still had change left over to buy an ice cream and a soda. Eddie's slightly older brother loved jigsaw puzzles, and he spent his entire shilling on a small ornamental box containing one thousand jigsaw pieces. The dark purple box was labelled 'One Thousand-Piece Mystery Jigsaw'.

As soon as Arthur got home, he emptied the box on to the floor of the front parlour, and started trying to piece the puzzle together. The wooden pieces were all backed in scarlet velvet, and were unlike any others that he had ever seen. It soon became clear that the jigsaw puzzle would be far harder to complete than the ones Arthur usually tackled, because the pieces did not seem to correspond to the picture on the box lid.

However, he persevered, and by eight o'clock that night he had completed a small section of the puzzle. It was a blonde girl, and her long hair covered her naked breasts. Arthur blushed deeply when he saw the figure, and wondered what the subject of the bizarre jigsaw puzzle would be when it was finished.

That evening, Arthur was playing cricket in Stanley Park when two giggling girls approached him. One of them was blonde, and her name was

Alice Crosby. Alice looked exactly like the blonde girl in the jigsaw puzzle. She ended up dating Arthur, and within a week, Arthur had lost his virginity to the girl. Alice started to help Arthur with the jigsaw puzzle, and, in turn, several intriguing and disturbing images were assembled. One showed a cloud, and what looked like bank-notes raining from it, whilst the other image showed a dreadful and disturbing scene – a child lying crushed under a huge cartwheel.

Two days later, a child in Everton was running alongside a cart as it rattled over the cobbles, when he stumbled and fell under the wheels. He died instantly from multiple injuries. Arthur and Alice heard about the terrible accident and suspected that it hadn't been a coincidence and were more determined than ever to complete the jigsaw puzzle. They wondered what the cloud of money signified, and they found out days later on the afternoon of Monday 27 July, as they enjoyed a day out in New Brighton.

Alice and Arthur were walking past New Brighton Tower, when suddenly, a shower of five-pound notes came fluttering down out of the sky. The young couple eagerly snatched handfuls of the money, which amounted to about sixty pounds. They thought it was a miracle, but they later discovered what had really happened when they read about it in the *Liverpool Echo*. As part of a publicity campaign, the publishers of *Titbits* magazine had thrown the money off New Brighton Tower. Hundreds of the magazine's readers had cut out a special coupon which allowed them into a cordoned-off area below the tower, where they were supposed to catch the five pound notes, but the unpredictable English weather had sabotaged the plan, and a rogue gust of wind had blown the notes away from the enclosure below the tower, towards Arthur and Alice.

The couple became more determined than ever to complete the mysterious jigsaw puzzle, but when they did so, they received a nasty shock. When the next pieces were assembled they made up a coffin and Arthur and Alice looked at each other in trepidation. Not long afterwards, Arthur's father, who had been perfectly fit and well, suddenly died.

Further strange disturbing scenes were pieced together. A figure that was unmistakably Arthur's older brother, George Ratcliffe, appeared in one scene wearing a military uniform. Many more scenes were put together, including a sinking liner, motorcars, rockets, planes and horrifying images of unspeakable, evil things. Alice became so afraid of the distressing images emerging from the jigsaw puzzle that she refused to go anywhere near it, and stopped going round to the Ratcliffe's house.

Young Edward stepped in to help Arthur finish the sinister puzzle, and ended up running to their mother in a state of terror. Mrs Ratcliffe went into the parlour and saw that the jigsaw puzzle was virtually complete. The various scenes and events within the puzzle formed a spiral, in the middle of which was a pallid, evil-looking face, which Mrs Ratcliffe immediately took to be the Devil. Without consulting the two boys, she fetched a brush and angrily began sweeping up the pieces of the puzzle. She shovelled them into the fire – but the pieces wouldn't burn, despite being made of wood.

So profound was the effect of the jigsaw on the two boys that both suffered nervous breakdowns and were said to have been committed to an asylum. Their older brother was killed in action in World War One, wearing the same uniform that the brothers had seen in the jigsaw puzzle six years before.

A STRANGE AFFAIR

A listener related the following story to me in 2003. I have had to change one or two basic details to avoid identifying the persons mentioned in the account.

In 1974, Reg, a wealthy middle-aged businessman from Gateacre, was married to twenty-five-year-old Audrey. People said the marriage would never work because of the twenty-five-year age difference, but Audrey and Reg seemed to be getting on very well during the first year of their marriage.

Reg owned a large factory near Litherland, and the business was bringing in more than enough money. He had a large house in Gateacre and was planning to buy another house in the country soon. Everything was looking rosy for Reg. He had a beautiful young wife, three cars, and a healthy bank balance, and things were going well for the newly-weds until Friday 13 September 1974.

As usual, Reg left home at 6.30am to get to the factory, and kissed his wife goodbye. However, he detected a certain coldness in her kiss. It wasn't a proper kiss. She just seemed to want to get it over and done with as quickly as possible before going back to sleep. This played on Reg's mind as he drove to the factory. He became so paranoid that he stopped the car halfway along the route – and turned back for home. He was convinced that Audrey was seeing someone else.

Determined to catch her unawares, he parked the car a short distance from the house, and crept up the path keeping close to the shrubbery, out of sight of the windows. He carefully inserted the key and silently turned it – then barged in. Audrey was upstairs having a shower, so she didn't hear him come in – and there were two champagne glasses on the coffee table in the lounge. Now Reg's suspicions were confirmed. He saw Audrey's lipstick on the rim of one glass, then he looked at the other, and held it carefully by the base of the stem. He could clearly see a man's thumb and fingerprint on the glass. He put the incriminating glass in his briefcase, then went upstairs. He could see Audrey in the shower cubicle through the frosted glass. There was no one with her. Reg crept around the other rooms of the house. There was no sign of anyone hiding anywhere. Consumed with jealousy and bitterness, he listened to Audrey singing in the shower for a moment or two, then silently left.

As he drove back to the factory, he unconsciously scowled and ground his teeth. It all made sense now: the missing cigar from his cigar box that he couldn't account for, the contraceptive pills Audrey was taking, even though she pretended to be broody. Lots of trivial little mysteries were now as clear as crystal. Audrey was definitely seeing someone. Reg wondered who it could possibly be. There was Terry, the young assistant manager at the factory. Reg had noticed how the young man had eyed Audrey when he had come round to dinner now and then, and Audrey was always asking about him. Then there was their neighbour, Roger, the handsome bachelor who had been to their house-warming party. It had to be one of them. Audrey had virtually no social life and only moved in very small circles. Everything was done for her, everything bought and fetched for her. It had to be Terry or Roger, Reg angrily assumed.

When Reg arrived at work, he was told that young Terry had called in to say that he was sick with 'flu. Reg was so paranoid that he raced round to Terry's home in Fazakerley and hammered on the door. Terry answered, still in his dressing gown and looking decidedly unwell, but Reg still quizzed him about his whereabouts that morning. Terry grumpily replied, "Where do you think I've been? I've been in bed, of course. I feel awful."

All the same, Reg was still suspicious and, determined to get hold of Terry's fingerprints, he asked him if he could use the toilet. When he was upstairs, Reg quickly grabbed a half-full glass of water from the bedside cabinet in Terry's bedroom, emptied it down the sink in the bathroom, then put it in his briefcase.

He left, and immediately set off to pay a visit to an old university friend, Tony Foster, who had once been a forensic science expert at a Home Office laboratory. He asked Foster to lift the prints off the champagne glass and drinking glass and compare them. Foster did so, but the prints did not match, leaving Reg feeling even more frustrated and perplexed.

Reg returned home to find that Audrey had cooked him his favourite lamb casserole and bought him a box of his favourite Don Carlos Presidente cigars, as well as an ivory Prometheus cigar lighter. Reg dismissed all her efforts as transparent attempts to divert attention from the affair he was convinced she was having. Still looking for her partner in adultery, he went next door and invited his neighbour Roger to dinner. Reg did the same trick – later that night he took the wine glass that Roger had been drinking from, and took it to his friend Foster. But again he had been barking up the wrong tree – Roger's fingerprints didn't match those on the champagne glass.

Reg cast his net wider and acquired more and more prints from other people whom he suspected of having an affair with Audrey, and still there was no match with the ones left on the champagne glass. Audrey, meanwhile, remained cool and distant distant, as if she was still seeing someone. It drove Reg to the verge of distraction.

One night he met an old friend, and went to Liverpool city centre with him for a drink. After his friend went home, Reg went on a bender, and ended up in Yates's Wine Lodge near the Blacklers store. He was so drunk by this time that he could hardly speak. This is where the story takes a supernatural twist …

… Reg suddenly collapsed – and 'died'.

He could hear the man who was feeling his pulse saying, "He's a gonner". He found himself in what he could later only describe as a black void. No matter which way he turned, there was nothing but infinite blackness.

Suddenly, at some point in this apparently timeless continuum, a figure in pale-looking clothes appeared and knelt by him. Reg was astounded to discover that it was his brother John who had been dead for over twenty years. Reg called his brother's name and asked where he was, and John simply said, "Eternity". Then he told Reg that he had bad news for him, he would have to go back to life again, his time had not yet come. Reg said that he didn't want to return, because he was heartbroken over Audrey having an affair. John gave him a very sympathetic look, then said, "It's the postman," and Reg hugged his brother with relief.

Reg woke up in hospital with his wife squeezing his hand. As soon as he opened his eyes, his first words were, "Audrey, why?"

His wife returned a puzzled look.

"It's the postman, isn't it?" Reg said.

Audrey looked aghast, and pretended she didn't know what he was talking about, but she later broke down and admitted to the affair. Reg immediately embraced her and they both sobbed – she apologising and promising never to stray again, and he forgiving her.

On the first day that he was discharged from hospital, he lay in wait for the unsuspecting postman. Behind the cover of the net curtains he watched him walk up the path towards the front door. Just as the postman reached the door, Reg opened it and grabbed him by the throat and threatened him.

Reg later discovered that the postman had a wife and children, which gave him even more ammunition, so he warned him that he'd reveal the affair to his wife unless he stopped seeing Audrey.

That did the trick.

Somehow, Reg and Audrey fell back in love and a year later Audrey gave birth to a baby boy, who was named John, after Reg's long-dead brother.

BED AND BREAKFAST GHOST

In February 2003 I received a call at Radio Merseyside from a listener called Jim who related a very intriguing tale about an ecclesiastical spectre that he had once encountered.

In 1993, Jim was divorced from his wife, and was therefore forced to seek alternative accommodation. His friend Tommy owned a recently opened bed-and-breakfast property in Anfield, opposite Liverpool's football ground, so Jim was given a temporary room there.

One evening, Jim entered the B&B and was about to walk up the stairs to his room, when he saw a strange-looking figure dressed in black, standing halfway up the stairs, blocking his way.

"He was wearing a wide, black, sombrero-type of hat and a short cape," Jim told me, recalling the eerie moment, "and he reminded me of the silhouetted figure of the man in black on the label of a Sandeman's Port bottle."

"Who are you? What do you want?" Jim nervously asked the figure, which slowly turned and walked silently up the stairs towards the landing where Jim's room was situated. Jim was fascinated and more than a little frightened, but curiosity got the better of him, and he cautiously ascended the stairs, wondering who, or what, he had just seen. When he opened the door to his room, he was startled to find the man in the black sombrero standing there, large as life, with his back to the fireplace. At this closer range, Jim could see that the man's attire looked like that once worn by the old pastors of Victorian and Edwardian times. Before he could decide what to do next, the figure vanished.

Jim lost no time in locating Tommy and urging him to tell him about the ghostly cleric – who was he? and what was he doing in his room?

"You've been drinking, Jimmy lad," was Tommy's view of the supernatural incident, but Jimmy angrily and repeatedly insisted that he had not imagined the man in black – he wasn't stupid. So the two men decided to research the history of the building which now housed the bed-and-breakfast, and they discovered that, in the nineteenth century, the premises had been a vicarage.

The solid-looking phantom of the minister continued to roam the B&B until the building was blessed by a clergyman, which is ironic, given that the ghost was that of a holy man.

VOICE ON THE RADIO

In November 2000, forty-year-old David Bradley, from Birkenhead, emerged from a bruising divorce feeling very depressed. He seemed to undergo a character change; he became melancholic and kept telling his friends he thought life was pointless.

Matthew, a friend of David's, was a very spiritual person, and he tried to persuade him that life wasn't as gloomy as he thought was. Things would improve.

One evening, Matthew took David to meet a Spiritualist in Liverpool, and she told him that Susan from the spirit world was very concerned about him. David was a bit startled, because his late mother's name had been Susan. Not even Matthew had known that. David asked her to describe his mother, and she described down to the last detail how Susan had looked while she had been on earth. David left the Spiritualist church feeling a little unnerved, but a part of him wondered if it had all been a confidence trick.

In early December 2000, David descended further into the depths of depression, and one morning at three o'clock he got out of bed and decided to get in to his car to drive a hundred miles to Nottingham. David had worked in the building trade in Nottingham almost ten years before, and at the time he had dated a girl called Alexandra. She had been the most beautiful and wonderful person he had ever met, but he had blown the relationship through his hard drinking. It had been the greatest regret of his life.

When he reached his former girlfriend's home he was told that no woman named Alexandra lived there. So he drove to a café, and after a meal, a cup of tea, and a smoke, he was back on the road, ready to return home, but he had to drive through Nottingham to reach the motorway. This was on the Saturday night of 16 December 2000. He turned on his radio, and was listening to a song by Craig David called *I'm Walking Away*, when, all of a sudden, a familiar-sounding female voice came from that radio, interrupting the song. The voice said, "David, don't turn right!"

David slowed the car, and glanced at the car radio, doubting his senses. That voice had not been heard for fifteen years, yet it was unmistakable. It was the soft, kindly voice of his mother, Susan Bradley.

David had intended to turn right, and he looked into his mirrors, ready to signal, but the voice came out of the radio once again, even more insistent this time. "David, don't turn right!" In that split second, he decided to obey the voice. He went straight on, but pulled over at the kerb. He sat there gazing at the car radio with a dumbfounded expression on his face. Seeking a logical explanation for what he had heard, he checked to see if there was a tape in the cassette player – there wasn't. Trembling, he lit a cigarette, and wound down the window to get some fresh air. He felt most peculiar and suspected that perhaps he really was having a nervous breakdown after all.

After about fifteen minutes, during which David tried to clear his head, he became aware of a distant wailing sound. It was heading in his direction. It was two police cars and an ambulance with their sirens screaming and their lights flashing. They hurtled past David and turned into the street – the very same street he was going into until the voice of his mother warned him not to.

Dreading the worst, David left his car, and slowly walked towards that street. What he saw as he turned the corner was to cure him of his depression. A car had mounted the pavement at a crazy angle and from under its crumpled bonnet, crushed against a brick wall, steam was still escaping. The driver was still inside the crashed vehicle, groaning in pain. A short distance beyond the crashed car, a young man was impaled on railings, his life rapidly ebbing away. His blood was dripping steadily down the railings as David looked on in horror. Dead on the pavement nearby, was a young woman, who would subsequently be identified as the girlfriend of the young man impaled on the railings. It was obvious to David that her legs and arms, and apparently her neck, were all broken. He stood there, rooted to the spot, as the full significance of the scene sank in, until the police pushed him back up the street, away from the carnage.

As he was driving home to Merseyside, he heard news of the crash on the radio. A man in Nottingham had been out drinking with friends. He had then driven home intoxicated and had travelled at fifty miles per hour in a built-up area, going the wrong way down a one-way street. The car had hit a barrier and had ploughed into two Nottingham Trent students; a young man and his girlfriend. Both had been killed in the accident.

The drunken driver had survived, despite crashing into the wall. He was convicted of drunken and dangerous driving and was later sent to prison for six years. Had David Bradley turned right into that one-way street, he would undoubtedly have been killed by the drunken driver in a head-on collision.

Two months after the crash, David was visiting a friend in Southport, and he literally bumped into his old flame, Alexandra. She had hardly changed and the same emotions he had felt ten years ago resurfaced and were reciprocated. As he no longer drank heavily, the relationship flourished, and in July 2001, the couple were married.

David is convinced that his mother loved him so much, that she somehow managed to return from beyond the grave to save his life on that bleak Saturday night in Nottingham.

MYSTERIOUS DOUBLE SHOOTING

In June 2002, I travelled to Runcorn's Bridge Street to look at the building that once housed the town's police station. I had been given permission to look around the basement of the former police station to see for myself the scene of one of the most baffling, almost supernatural, crimes of the last century.

In 1929, the basement served as a storeroom for guns and ammunition, and in April of that year it was the scene of a double shooting which ended with the death of a police superintendent and his son.

In April 1929, thirty-one-year-old Reverend Frank Hayward left St Mary's Parish Church in Ormskirk to travel to his parents' home in Runcorn. His fiancée, a Miss Margaret Mackintosh, accompanied him on the visit. Frank's father was fifty-six-year-old Superintendent Charles Hayward of the Cheshire Constabulary, and he was based at Runcorn Police Station. Frank was the apple of his father's eye, and the superintendent listened proudly when his son told him that he intended to build his own church soon.

During the weekend, at around half past eleven, Superintendent Hayward took his son into Runcorn Police Station to show him the gun-room in the basement, where several high-powered rifles, ten revolvers and nearly four hundred rounds of ammunition were kept. This hardware had been surrendered to the officers over the years, but was not used by the police themselves. Frank was due to return to his church in Ormskirk after the visit, and so had changed into his clerical attire. Meanwhile, his fiancée was packing her case in the superintendent's home, which adjoined the station.

Upstairs at the desk was acting sergeant, Frederick Bell. No one else was about in the station. At half-past noon he heard a loud bang which came from the gun-room, followed by the superintendent yelling out Bell's name. The acting sergeant ran pell-mell down the steps to find out what had happened. Superintendent Hayward was obviously in deep shock and stammered, "Bell … Bell … something terrible has happened! My son … Frank … picked up the revolver … he didn't know anything was in it … and …and … it … it went off before I knew what had happened."

Nearby, the Reverend Hayward lay on the floor with blood pouring from a bullet-hole above his right eye. The superintendent was holding a revolver in his left hand – the revolver that had killed his son. "Telephone for Doctor Murphy," Superintendent Hayward urged him, so Bell ran upstairs, but before he could even dial the number, another shot rang out. Bell raced back downstairs to the gun-room and found the superintendent lying dead on the floor, with a gunshot wound just above his right ear.

It was deduced that Reverend Hayward had picked up a revolver and it had accidentally gone off, killing him instantly. Then, his father, filled with remorse at the shock of losing his beloved son, had committed suicide. However, facts uncovered at the inquest made this theory look unlikely. The bullet that had killed Frank had entered his head at an angle from above, and the revolver muzzle had been very close when it was fired. Frank had been stooping when he was shot, and the angle of the bullet entering the superintendent's head was also suspect. However, the jury still returned a verdict of Frank's death being accidental while his father's had been a suicide.

Sergeant Bell had been in the storeroom shortly before the superintendent and his son had arrived. He testified that he had checked that the firearms were safe – yet someone had taken two bullets from a carton and then placed them in the gun which had killed the Reverend Frank Hayward and his father. The primary witness statement in this case came from the mouth of Sergeant

Bell, which leads me to regard him with a suspicious eye. Did he have something to do with the deaths? If so, what could his motive possibly have been? Did the death of Superintendent Hayward result in Sergeant Bell being promoted? Or, could Bell have been having an affair with Mrs Hayward, and had she perhaps decided that she wanted her husband out of the way? The police surely checked all such possibilities.

The double shooting at Runcorn Police Station remains a tantalising puzzle. I leave it to you to formulate a credible explanation.

THE GHOSTLY CHARIOTEER

The subject of the following story is an apparition which I am unable to identify. Many people have encountered it over the years, although I still haven't a clue whose ghost it is, but perhaps you do, and if so, please write to me, care of my publishers (details at the end of book).

In the 1930s, the 6A tram ran from Bowring Park to the Pier Head, and this was the tram which two twenty-one-year-old lads, Teddy and Bert, boarded to take them to a ball on Edge Lane. The ball continued until one in the morning, and when Teddy kissed his sweetheart from Edge Hill goodnight, he and Bert had to set off home on foot, as there were no trams running at that hour. The homeward journey of over three miles was not too arduous, since it was a warm night and they had the light of the moon to show the way, and they were both feeling cheery from the wine they had consumed at the ball.

As the men reached the green open spaces of Bowring Park, they intended to go their separate ways, as Teddy lived in Huyton, and Bert lived near Page Moss, but as they were saying goodnight to one another, they heard what seemed to be the distant sound of a galloping horse. They halted in their tracks and strained their ears, and realised that the horse was heading in their direction, because the strangely echoing sound of its hooves was steadily increasing in volume. What the two men saw next sobered them up in a flash and impressed an indelible memory on their minds.

Approaching them was the spectral figure of a woman, with long hair that fluttered and flowed in the breeze as she rode a horse-drawn chariot. The phantom charioteer crossed the moonlit field at high speed, coming within thirty feet of Ted and Bert, before vanishing into the night air. The rattle of the chariot wheels and the thunder of galloping hooves quickly diminished, seconds after the alarming vision faded.

Bert was so terrified that he refused to go home alone in the direction of Page Moss, because that was the direction in which the striking apparition seemed to have been headed. He therefore stayed at Teddy's home, and throughout the rest of that night, the two men hardly spoke a word. Both of them had a chilling, albeit irrational conviction that the phantom charioteer had been some harbinger of death and disaster.

A week later, Bert's mother died in her sleep for no apparent reason.

Not long after that, Teddy started work at Cronton Colliery, and in a freak accident, he lost four of his fingers after getting his sleeve snagged in machinery at the plant there. Both men believed the supernatural encounter at Bowring Park had been a warning of death and misfortune.

As Teddy was recovering at home from his accident, a neighbour happened to mention that several people in the Huyton area had recently seen the ghost of the long-haired woman driving a chariot at breakneck speed over Bowring Park. Neither Teddy nor Bert had mentioned a word to anyone about the apparition, so that ruled out a practical joke.

There were to be many more sightings of the female charioteer during the hours of darkness.

At nine o'clock on the Thursday night of Halloween, 1974, two twelve-year-old girls were crossing a field at Bowring Park, on their way home from a duck-apple party at a friend's house, when they heard the thunderous sound of a galloping horse's hooves. They stopped in their tracks and soon saw a horse come hurtling out of the darkness, the chariot it pulled narrowly missing them as it flew past, the wheels throwing up dirt and stones. Both girls clearly saw the woman holding the reins of the horse, apparently oblivious to their presence. In a repeat of her previous appearances, the phantom charioteer crossed the field at high speed, then vanished into the darkness, and the girls ran all the way home in a state of terror.

It would seem that sightings of the magnificent ghostly charioteer of Bowring Park date back to the nineteenth century, but who she is remains a mystery.

A few years ago, what seems to have been the same ghost was seen further afield – near Speke. At the time of the sighting, the M57 was being extended and the excavations uncovered a previously unknown Roman hunting lodge, so it was conjectured that the spectral charioteer probably dated back to Roman times.

INVISIBLE BODYGUARD

The following story was related to me by Dawn, a thirty-eight-year-old mother of three who lives in Heswall.

In 1977, Dawn was a very lonely child of thirteen living in the Anfield district of Liverpool. Her parents had divorced and were living separate lives, and Dawn had decided to live with her Auntie Vera, who worked in a local shop.

In 1977, Dawn and her aunt moved into an old house near County Road, and Dawn soon realised that the building had ghosts. On the first night, she was awakened by the sensation of someone sitting on the end of her bed. She looked up, and saw the shadowy outline of what seemed to be a boy of about her own age, but he wore old-fashioned clothes, and she could distinctly see his white, high, shirt collar and white cuffs. Although the ghostly boy did nothing to alarm her, Dawn ducked under the blankets for several minutes, before slowly re-emerging to peep over the covers. The spectre of the boy had gone. The next morning Dawn told her aunt, but Vera dismissed it as nothing more than a bad dream, probably induced by eating a large helping of cheese on toast before bed.

On the following Sunday evening at around 8.30pm, Vera went to visit a friend, and while she was out, a terrifying incident occurred in the old house. Dawn was reading a comic, when suddenly, she heard thumping sounds coming from the rooms upstairs, like the heavy tread of someone walking about. She froze as she heard the footsteps clumping down the stairs. She bolted for the hallway, and it was here that she saw the ghost that would give her nightmares for years to come. A hugely obese woman, dressed like a Victorian maid, was standing on the stairs. She had a round, plump face, and her hair was piled up into an untidy bun. In her hand she held a large carving knife, and there was streaks of wet, glistening blood on her white apron. The woman looked at Dawn with an expression of pure hatred, and without warning, she came lumbering down the stairs towards her.

Dawn scrambled for the front door in a frantic attempt to escape, but she forgot that her Aunt Vera had told her to put the door bolt on while she was out. She shrieked as the vast shadow of the menacing woman lunged towards her as she fumbled desperately with the bolt. She felt her snatching at her long hair as she finally managed to slide back the bolt. She finally yanked open the door and ran into the street, completely distraught.

Dawn's tale was not believed by anybody, and Vera even arranged for a doctor to examine her to see if she was suffering from some kind of mental illness. Unable to determine any specific condition, he prescribed a general tonic for the child's nerves. She was obviously troubled because of her parent's divorce, he said. But not long afterwards, the menacing ghost of the corpulent maid returned. She appeared, as before, on the stairs, but on this occasion, she merely scowled and shook her fist before vanishing.

One night Dawn woke up with a start after feeling cold lips kissing her hand. She looked up and saw the phantom boy looking over her. This time she was too sleepy to be afraid, and simply asked, "Who are you?" The boy smiled, then vanished into the darkness without a sound. He appeared more and more frequently, with almost clockwork regularity, and was apparently something of an invisible bodyguard, because on one occasion when Dawn went to step out in front of a car which she hadn't noticed, she felt unseen hands pull her back to the kerb. On another occasion she left bread unattended under the grill and a voice out of nowhere called her name in the kitchen to alert her to the fire hazard.

One afternoon, the ghostly maid with the blood-stained apron reappeared on the stairs and proceeded to chase Dawn wielding a knife, when the phantom boy appeared between the big woman and Dawn, and wrestled with her. Dawn yelled out in horror as she saw the woman stab the boy, but the knife produced no blood, and the boy suffered no injury. The woman and the boy then vanished. After that, the knife-wielding woman never reappeared.

Several days later, something particularly strange took place at the haunted house. Dawn rushed home from school one day to watch her favourite children's television programme; a serial called *Midnight is a Place*. As she sat on the sofa watching the programme, she felt a hand gently squeezing hers, and she sensed the presence of someone sitting beside her. Gradually, the faint outline of the boy appeared. Children don't always react to ghosts the way adults do, and Dawn bravely asked the boy once again who he was. "David," he said coyly. He was a very shy young lad. His hair had a centre part and he had the pale angelic face of a choirboy. He had obviously fallen for Dawn, and the unusual love between the boy from the spirit world and the girl from the land of the living seemed to intensify as the days went by.

One day, Aunt Vera happened to gaze through the window, and she also saw the strange boy sitting on the sofa beside Dawn, but when she went into the house, he had vanished. When questioned, Dawn blushed and explained that the boy had actually been a ghost. Vera was horrified by the way Dawn was speaking, and she had the house blessed by a priest. Then a medium was consulted and visited the house. She said that a back-street abortionist called Mary O'Leary was haunting the house, as well as the ghost of a boy from a later Edwardian period, although the psychic could not ascertain his name. Dawn knew though.

The ghost of David gradually visited less frequently, and at the age of fourteen, Dawn started to see Danny, a flesh-and-blood boyfriend. One night she awoke to find a single red rose on her pillow. She clutched it, knowing immediately who it was from, but by morning it was nowhere to be seen, and David never visited her again.

CANNING STREET GHOST

In the Spring of 1996, Ben and Chloe, a couple from St Helen's, moved into a newly furnished apartment situated on the second floor of a Georgian house on Canning Street in Liverpool city centre. They were the first tenants in the entire house since the premises had been renovated, and on the first night after the couple had moved in, strange things began to happen. A very sweet scent pervaded the living room around midnight, and the sounds of someone walking slowly up the stairs from the bottom flight to the top could be heard. Ben was so sure that an intruder was outside the door, that he shouted, "Who's there?" And in reply, something rapped three times on the door. When Ben bravely, or perhaps unwisely, opened the door, he found that there was no one there.

One night, about a week later, Chloe was sitting in bed reading a book by the light of a bedside lamp, when an incident occurred which almost paralysed her with fear. The tall black figure of a man stepped right out of the solid wall by her bed. He wore a top hat and a long cape, but although his shirt and collar were white, his neck, face and hands were as black and featureless as a silhouette. He picked up the glass of water from the bedside cabinet, lifted it to the ovoid blackness of his face, sipped it, then put it back on the cabinet. He then turned so swiftly that his cape swirled in a semi-circle behind him, and he then melted back into the wall from which he had emerged seconds before.

When Ben returned home from work at nine o'clock, he found Chloe standing outside on the steps of the house, trembling and sobbing. It took him a long time to persuade her to go back into their flat. When she showed him the drinking glass from which the ghost had sipped, she let out a yelp of revulsion and slammed it back down on the cabinet as though it were alive. On the rim of the glass was a silvery, sticky residue, as fine as a cobweb.

Ben later took that glass to be examined by two university students who had said they were studying parapsychology. They intended to have the weird residue analysed but the specimen had somehow evaporated from its sealed container before they could get it to a laboratory. A fortnight later, the so-called parapsychologists ran screaming from the haunted flat on Canning Street after a freezing, invisible hand had stroked both their faces.

One Friday night, Chloe intended to go out on the town with several work-mates, but refused to shower unless one of her friends stood guard outside the shower cubicle in the haunted apartment. Chloe's friend Sam laughingly agreed to keep watch outside the shower unit reading a magazine. Some time later, Chloe heard a loud bump, so she switched off the shower, wiped the water from her eyes, and through the frosted glass of the shower unit she could make out someone in black standing there. It was unmistakably the outline of the top-hatted ghost. Chloe let out a high-pitched scream, and the figure vanished.

When she ventured outside the shower unit, she found the door wide open. Her friend Sam had apparently also seen the materialisation of the ghost, and had been rendered speechless and charged straight out of the house. Sam never returned to that apartment and still refuses to go anywhere near Canning Street. However, there were two more terrifying incidents still to come.

Just under a month later, Chloe and Ben were in bed one night, when Ben went to fetch a snack from the kitchen. Chloe relaxed back in the bed, and yawned. She stretched up her arms and yawned again, and as she did so, a pair of icy hands came from behind the headboard of the bed – and seized her tightly by the wrists. When she looked up, she saw the same ink black shadow of a face peering down at her. This time she was so petrified that she lost consciousness. When she came round, she was on the sofa in the living room, and Ben declared that enough was enough. They were leaving. They could spend the night in his uncle's house in Crosby – they would not spend another night in the haunted flat. At three in the morning, the couple snatched up a few possessions, climbed into their brand new Honda Accord, and drove off.

As the car was travelling down Parliament Street, they became aware of the same sweet scent that had pervaded their apartment just before all the supernatural trouble had started. The driving-wheel in Ben's hands suddenly turned left by itself, as if someone with terrific strength was twisting it. The car veered left and mounted the kerb on the corner of Windsor Street. Ben somehow managed to regain control of the vehicle, and luckily no pedestrians were about at that hour. Convinced he was back in control, Ben continued down Chaloner Street towards Wapping, when once again something powerful turned the steering wheel sharply left. This time, the Honda swerved violently down a road past the Salthouse Dock. The accelerator pedal was being pressed down by an invisible force, and even though Ben had taken his foot off the clutch, the car refused to stall.

The car was about to turn down the sloping ramp leading into the dock, when Ben yanked on the handbrake in a last-ditch attempt to stop the possessed vehicle, and the car screeched, turned through 180 degrees, and eventually stopped dead. Ben told Chloe to leave the vehicle and stand well out of harm's way, and he drove the Honda to a car park and abandoned it. He and Chloe then hailed a taxi which took them to Crosby, and even in the taxi, the malevolent spirit wouldn't give in. The taxi swerved, and the cabby apologised, saying the hackney cab's steering seemed to be "wonky", even though he knew for a fact that there was nothing wrong with the vehicle.

Ben and Chloe still can't understand why the malicious ghost victimised them, but I have heard many other accounts of the Canning Street ghost which haunts their former address. I think he is the spirit of some stern Victorian gentleman who resents people living in what he considers to be *his* old house.

WELSH WITCH

In October 1900, Richard Anderton of Almonds Green, West Derby, took his wife and children to stay with relatives in Flint for a fortnight. In those days, such an undertaking was a great adventure and a great treat for their three children. They had a wonderful time playing in the fields with their cousins and enjoying a much greater level freedom than they were normally allowed in Liverpool.

The day before the Andertons were due back in Liverpool, their youngest son, six-year-old Oliver, vanished while playing hide-and-seek with his two cousins near a deserted old cottage. Oliver's cousins told police that they had heard a whooshing noise coming from high above their heads at about the time he went missing, but their story was dismissed as a confused childish fantasy.

Richard Anderton stayed behind in Flint, determined to find his son, while his traumatised wife and two children returned home to West Derby. As they trudged up the lane to their house after their long journey, they were shocked to find young Oliver, sitting on the doorstep of the house, as large as life, apparently no worse for his experience. The tale that the youngster told his mother and two sisters was a very strange one indeed.

He said that while he had been playing outside in Flint, a tall old woman in black had touched his head and he had found himself unable to move, or cry out. She took him to a strange-looking house in the middle of nowhere, and then told him she was going to keep him as her stepson. Not surprisingly, Oliver started crying, and the old woman scolded him severely, which only made him worse. He cried and cried and cried.

Later that night she could take no more of his crying, so with an impatient sigh she took him outside, wrapped him a blanket and held him tightly in her arms as she flew off into the night! Oliver was only six years of age, yet he is said to have drawn what he saw during his airborne journey home to Liverpool: the distinctive shape of the Wirral peninsula as it looks from the air.

The Andertons tried to rationalise the bizarre incident, but were ultimately unable to explain their son's mysterious fifteen-mile journey home. They were just grateful that he had returned to them safe and well.

EXECUTION IN A RAILWAY TUNNEL

Heswall housewife Maria Cunningham will never forget the Halloween of 1996. Maria visited London with her twelve-year-old son, Jason. In the morning they went to Madam Tussaud's and later paid a visit to her sister in the London district of Kensington.

Just after nine o'clock that night, Maria and her son boarded the London to Liverpool train at Euston Station. As the train entered a tunnel, Maria, Jason, and several other passengers, were startled and horrified to see the flashing image of a man convulsing in the throes of death in an electric chair, just beyond the window-panes of the railway carriage. The disturbing image could not have been projected on to the wall of the tunnel by some hoaxer, because the witnesses all agreed that the man in the chair had looked three-dimensional and completely solid. The deeply disturbing image had been so detailed and vivid, that Mrs Cunningham had even seen sparks of electricity around the metal wristbands fastening the man to the chair. The same terrifying apparition was later seen by tourist in the same railway tunnel in 1999.

The electric chair has never been used in Britain, but there are rumours that a London gangster was tortured in an access tunnel off that stretch of railway line in the 1950s. It is alleged that he was wired to an electrical transformer to make him talk.

When I gave out an account of this strange story on the radio, I received a call from a man called Freddy Ryden. In 2000, Freddy and four friends decided to go to London to look for work in the construction industry, and minutes before their train pulled into Euston, they all saw the distinct image of a man bound by metal bracelets to what seemed to be an electric chair. On this occasion, the man's face was obscured by a dark vapour, but Freddy and his friends could clearly see the body violently convulsing as sparks fizzed from the bracelets on his hands.

The Liverpool men informed a guard about the electrocuted man as soon as the train pulled into the station, but the guard said that it was impossible for anyone to be sitting in a chair in that stretch of tunnel, as there were simply no vaults or passages where the figure could be situated.

To deepen the mystery further, I recently received a newspaper cutting about the ghost in the electric chair, published in the *Daily Mirror* in the late 1990s. Here is the gist of the article:

A twenty-two-year-old Watford housewife, Karen Woo, was taking the tube to London for a spot of sightseeing with her family and her eight-year-old nephew Kaitian, when she decided to take his photograph. Only after the snapshots had been developed did Karen realise that she had captured a strange apparition on film. Behind her nephew, framed by the window of the tube train, in the inky blackness of the tunnel, was the clear image of a man being executed in an electric chair. Karen said, "My husband's family was visiting from Malaysia and wanted a picture of them all travelling on a tube train. I had the photos developed a few months later and was completely astounded because I'd never seen anything like it before. I'm not one for believing in anything weird … but …"

So many independent witnesses, all describing the same apparition, lend weight and credibility to the sightings, and we can only speculate as to their significance.

Journeys of the Mind

One miserable night in February 1950, Alf, a quiet and very inoffensive man aged about seventy, was having supper in the old Sailors' Home in Liverpool. For years he had told anyone who would listen about his adventures at sea in the regular Navy and the Merchant Navy, and most of his listeners had automatically assumed that Alf was telling the truth. However, on this particular night, a man named George, who had spent most of his life at sea, confronted Alf over one of his claims.

Alf had mentioned that he had served on the *Empress of India* under Admiral Beattie, but George had served on that same ship, and he certainly had no recollection of Alf being onboard. For a while, Alf persisted in his claim, but finally was forced to admit that he hadn't. He had never even served in the British Navy, or the Merchant Navy for that matter, because all his life he had suffered from epilepsy, and no naval service would have him. His illness had made life difficult for a man who had come from a seafaring family which could claim ancestors in Nelson's Navy.

In 1860, the Sailors' Home on Canning Street caught fire, and several men were trapped in the upper floors of the building. They leaned out of the windows, frantically crying out for help, but when a ladder was raised to the trapped men, it was seen to be too short to reach them. A brave young sailor in the crowd rushed up the ladder, despite the cries of the police urging him to come back down. This man was William, Alf's father. He stood on the top rung of the ladder, and gripped the window ledge.

"Come on!" William shouted to the men, who were choking with the smoke and fumes which were billowing out of the window.

One by one, the men climbed out of the window and scrambled over the brave sailor's body and on to the ladder. Then William screamed as the flames suddenly rushed up from the window below and burnt his legs and face, scarring him for life. All the same, he managed to get back down the ladder, and was hailed as the hero of the day.

Twenty years later, in 1880, Alf was born, the ninth son of William. Every other son had gone into the Navy, or served on a ship, but Alf began to suffer fits when he was ten years of age. It soon became clear that he would never go to sea to make a living, even though it was in his blood. Alf's father virtually disowned him, ashamed to have a son who couldn't follow in his footsteps.

As well as listening to his father and his brothers, he had learned about the sea from reading books. He knew about every naval battle, every tale of disasters at sea, and related vivid accounts of them as if he had been there in person, yet in reality, he had never even ventured as far as the Isle of Man.

The sailors in the home were amazed when they found out the truth about Alf, and many of them felt conned and quite foolish. In particular, they thought about Alf's gripping maritime tales as first mate onboard a ship called the *Washington Queen*. Each night over cocoa and rum, Alf would spin a salty yarn about adventures he had experienced aboard the *Washington Queen*, and how he had roamed the seven seas on board that ship. Had all that been a tissue of lies as well? they asked him. Alf insisted that there really was a ship called the *Washington Queen*, and tears rolled down his face. He went on to say that it was his own ship, but no one believed him now and one by one, each sailor turned his back on him. No one told the old man to go, but he felt so ashamed at being caught out as a liar, that he packed his few belongings, and left the Sailors' Home just after midnight.

Feeling utterly miserable and dejected, he wandered through the freezing February night, down the frigid, deserted streets of the city, towards the old landing stage at the Pier Head, perhaps to reflect on a life that he had yearned for, but which had been denied him by a cruel illness. That was where he was last seen alive.

On the following morning, a group of children came upon Alf's cold, stiff body in Shaw Street Park, lying huddled up inside a wooden longboat in a sandpit. He was inadequately covered by a thin layer of crumpled newspapers, and a post-mortem established that he had died from hypothermia.

One of Alf's friends later visited the park to see the place where he had died and to pay his respects. He went to the children's play area and came upon the wooden longboat in the sand. As he drew near, he suddenly noticed the words *Washington Queen* scrawled in faded paint along the side of the land-locked boat, and he realised that he was looking at the ship that had taken Alf on so many seafaring journeys of the imagination.

It was said that not long after Alf's death, his ghost was often seen in Shaw Street Park, gently smiling at groups of children playing at being sailors in the old wooden boat.

PREMONITION OF DEATH IN BOOTLE

Regular readers of my books will know that I have often written about premonitions. A premonition is a glimpse of the future, and it can manifest itself as a very strong and seemingly irrational 'hunch', or gut-feeling about something, or it can even make itself known in a dream. Premonitions have taken the form of warning voices and alarming visual apparitions, but most of the cases I have looked into over the years have concerned dreams.

I once read of an intriguing account of a premonition experienced by the writer Rudyard Kipling – a man who was very sceptical about the supernatural. In his autobiography, Kipling relates how he once had a dream in which he saw himself standing in a line of formally dressed men. In the dream he noticed that he was in a huge, stone-floored hall in which there was some sort of ceremony in progress, but he could not see the proceedings, because a large crowd blocked his view. The dream continued for what seemed quite some time, then a stranger approached, took hold of Rudyard's arm, and said, "I want a word with you." At that point, Kipling woke up with the dream still vividly in his mind. He wondered for a while about the unusually realistic dream, then forgot about it.

Six weeks later, Rudyard was attending a war memorial service in Westminster Abbey, when he gradually recognised the setting as that which had formed the backdrop to his dream. He stood in his pew and glanced at the men on each side of him. They were exactly the same men he had seen in his dream. Rudyard knew what was coming next. A stranger approached, took his arm, and said: "I want a word with you."

"How, or why, had I been shown an unreleased roll of my life in film. What was the significance of the short scene?" Kipling later mused.

Do premonitions of the sort experienced by Kipling hint that our lives are already mapped out in the finest detail from cradle to grave? That would mean that we are like someone walking in the snow, not only leaving footprints behind, but also stepping into ones already made by our fate. If Kipling had deliberately avoided going to Westminster Abbey, would he have created a paradox? Because, if he had pretended to be ill to avoid going to the scene of his premonition, that would have proved that he had a choice to dodge a future event he had glimpsed through a premonition. However, it is curious that Kipling only realised he was living the premonitory dream once he was actually attending the service in Westminster Abbey.

~

One snowy January night in the winter of 1946, Sam Jepson, an elderly Bootle widower, sipped a small measure of milk laced with rum, before climbing the two flights of stairs to his bedroom. Mr Jepson snuggled down in his bed to get warm and from there he watched the flitting shadows of large snowflakes thrown by the streetlamps down across the curtains of his window. He was soon asleep, but as he slept, he had a weird, disturbing dream which left him paralysed with fear.

The nightmare began with the face of a helmeted man in the cockpit of an aeroplane, and then the dreadful whining sound of the plane going into a steep dive. The pilot's eyes were wide open with shock, and he was trying desperately to pull the plane up from its doomed descent. The scene then changed to a familiar street in Bootle – St John's Road – which was about two hundred yards away from his home. The plane was hurtling down out of the sky – and seemed destined to crash land in a street where some children were playing.

Mr Jepson froze in utter terror in his bed, unable to awaken and so avoid the terrifying nightmare. He could hear his heart pounding as he held his breath and awaited the impact. The plane crashed with a thunderous explosion and an enormous fireball swept down the length street. The flames reached the children and they all fell over, then debris and fragments of the plane flew everywhere, smashing windows and shaking houses to their foundations.

Sam Jepson woke up at last and sprang up from his pillow with sweat pouring from his forehead.

His ordeal was to be but the first of six nightmares; each of them identical in every horrifying detail to the one before. In the end, the tormented old man went to a police station and told a constable about the dreams, and how he had interpreted them as a premonition. The constable was rather bemused. He was accustomed to dealing with burglaries, wife-beatings, theft, motoring offences, missing children and pets – but premonitions? He advised the old man to see his doctor, who might prescribe a tonic. Mr Jepson left in a huff. The constable hook his head and smirked at the old man's silly tale.

On the morning of 12 February 1946, twenty-four-year-old Canadian test pilot, Thomas Wilson Wall, climbed into the cockpit of a Firefly fighter plane and took off from the Royal Canadian Naval air station at Burscough. Lieutenant Wall performed several aeronautical manoeuvres over the skies of the North West, until a thick mist descended which hampered his aerial acrobatics. According to the *Liverpool Echo*, the single-seater fighter plane had apparently been performing a power drive when it went out of control and plunged into a nose-dive – directly over the streets of Bootle.

That morning, John Hudson, a postman from Smeaton Street, Kirkdale, was on his bicycle delivering parcels on St John's Road in Bootle. Further down the street, the three children of a Mrs Jacobs were playing games. They were Irene, aged five, her three-year-old brother Frank, and their twenty-month-old baby brother, Arthur, gurgling in his playpen. Sam Jepson was in a shop several streets away when he suddenly realised that his recurrent nightmare was about to become reality. The steady scream of an, as yet, unseen aeroplane in trouble, echoed through the cloudy skies over Bootle. People stopped what they were doing and looked to the heavens in dread. The whining lowered in pitch and the dark outline of the fighter plane zoomed down out of the low clouds towards the houses like a gigantic arrow – straight towards St John's Road.

The plane narrowly missed the chimney stack of the nearby saw manufacturers and impacted into the road, burying it's nose-cone eight feet into the ground. There was a tremendous explosion which threw Postman Hudson off his bike, leaving him severely burned on the face and hands. The fireball expanded and swept down the street like an enormous fiery balloon, hitting Mrs Jacobs' children. Irene received the most serious burns, and later died from toxaemia and shock at Bootle General Hospital. Hundreds of people poured out into the streets as their homes shook from the crash. By a strange twist of fate, many more children and their teachers would have suffered death and injury if St John's School had still been standing, because it had been situated just feet away from the point of impact. However, the school had been blitzed in the war a few years previously.

Within minutes, the military descended on the crash scene, led by an officer named Catterall, who surveyed the wreckage and quickly noticed that the pilot had baled out just before the plane had crashed. The uninjured pilot came down, light as a feather, on his parachute near Queen's Road.

Sam Jepson felt as if he was sleepwalking. With ambulances wailing and adults and children screaming, he wandered past the smouldering, twisted metal fragments of the plane to the knot of military personnel and bystanders standing by the remains of the Firefly. One of the policemen who was present was the very same one he had visited that wintry night to tell him about the dreams of a plane crash that wouldn't go away. The constable gave him a

113

knowing look, then nodded, as if to say, "Yes, you were right."

After that fateful February day, and despite the horrific scenes he had witnessed in St John's Road, Mr Jepson was haunted no more by the menacing dreams which had foretold a plane crash.

MESSAGE FROM THE GLASS

In the 1970s, a group of seven Liverpool University students lodged together at a house on Liverpool's Edge Lane. One evening, one of the students was mooching about up in the attic, when he found an old Edwardian ouija board, and it wasn't long before he and his friends were experimenting with the upturned glass on the board. Their seven index fingers rested on the inverted wine-glass, and, unlike most people who dabble with the ouija board for amusement, the students took what they were doing very seriously. The time was eleven o'clock at night, and a single candle lit the room.

After a few moments, the glass started to move steadily, and the students noted that it was sliding towards the letter 'C'. Then it moved to the letter 'H'. Within thirty seconds the name 'Charlie' had been spelled out. One of the students looked uneasily around the darkened room, and in a sombre voice said, "Hello Charlie". The glass seemed to jolt, as if the force moving it was excited. One of the students, a young man who was rather frightened by the proceedings, got up and walked over to the light switch. He clicked the switch – but the light wouldn't go on. He clicked it again and again, but the light bulb still refused to shine, so the youth had no choice but to rejoin his friends, feeling rather uneasy. There was just one finger remaining on the glass, and as it slid about the board, the other students noted the garbled message it spelt out. It was a person's name, followed by the two words, 'murdered me'. Then came three more words, 'I was hanged'. The students assumed that they were conversing with a spirit from the age of capital punishment, which they knew had ended in the 1960s.

Moments later, another spirit came through, and this spirit was very mischievous, because it initially claimed that it was the deceased uncle of one of the female students, and it even seemed to know all the details about her uncle's life. However, the presence started spelling out obscene words and even claimed the girl would 'die nasty' when she was thirty. The students ended up fleeing from the flat, and as they did so, a shadowy hand appeared in mid-air and pinched the candle's wick, plunging the room into darkness. When they later returned to the room with torches, they found the impressions of tooth-marks in the candle.

When the landlord heard about the ouija's information regarding the spirit, Charlie, and the message about being hanged, he cast his mind back to a mysterious murder that had taken place just a few doors away, at Number 62 Edge Lane, in 1946.

At around ten o'clock on the Saturday night of 2 February 1946, fourteen-year-old Ernest Johnson from Number 13 Watford Road, in Anfield, decided to call upon his cousin Charles Greeney, the eleven-year-old son of Mrs Greeney, a money-lender, and Charles, a plasterer. When Ernest Johnson arrived at Number 62, he found that the front door was open, and all the lights were on in the large, eleven-room house. The place had been ransacked and it was obvious that there had been a break-in.

When Ernest looked in the kitchenette, he found the schoolboy, Charlie Greeney, hanging by his neck from the clothes rack, and he seemed to be dead. Ernest ran out of the house and informed the neighbours next door about the murder. He then rushed just two-hundred yards to a hotel where the dead boy's parents were having their usual Saturday evening drink. The parents returned to the house and the father took Charlie down from the rack and tried to give him a drink to resuscitate him, but it was no use. He was dead.

The value of property that had been taken from the house was valued at six hundred pounds. Expensive clocks, a huge fawn Wilton carpet, brand new suits, fur coats and various other expensive items had been stolen, but the safe in the office where Mrs Greeney carried out her money-lending business was untouched. The family's seven-month-old bull terrier pup was in the yard outside the kitchen where the hanging had taken place, and although the pup barked whenever strangers called, the neighbours said he had not made a sound that night. The only clue to the burglary and murder was a plain Albion van that had been seen parked on Dorothy Street, just around the corner from the house. Chief Superintendent Fothergill wondered if the burglars had been recognised by Charlie, and they had killed him to ensure he remained silent. Or, as another detective suggested, had the burglars broken into the house and found the boy hanging as they were ransacking the place?

Five men were soon arrested for the burglary and four of them were also held on suspicion of murder. A sixth man was arrested in Gibraltar. All four swore they had not killed Charlie Greeney. Two of the men said that when they broke into the house, they saw Charlie apparently standing on a chair in front of a fireplace with his back towards them. He was not moving, and they at first assumed he was deaf, so they proceeded to burgle the other rooms. The inquest proved that Charlie could not have hanged himself and hoisted his own body up on to the clothes rack, but the investigation eventually ground to a frustrating halt.

The four accused men were found not guilty of murder. The judge summed up the strange case by saying, "Although we are not certain that it was an accident, we are not certain that it was not." The hanging of Charles Greeney is therefore still an unsolved mystery.

The seven students who communicated with the spirit of Charlie – who said he had died by being hanged – were from Wiltshire, Leeds and Hull, and they knew nothing of the Greeney murder case of 1946. Was it all coincidence and hysteria, or did the spirit of the deceased schoolboy try to contact the living to identify his murderer?

THE MESSAGE

In the early 1990s, Amy, an ambitious twenty-year-old from Kirkby, decided to apply for a job in the United States as a proof-reader and sub editor with a magazine based in Greenwich Village, New York City. Everyone said Amy stood no chance of getting the job, but the letter she sent to the company was regarded as being so original and honest, that she was invited over to New York to work for a trial period. Amy got on so well that she ended up being employed at the publishing house and later obtained a green card.

She married a New Yorker in 1995, but ended up divorced through irreconcilable differences by the year 2000.

In the year 2001, on Valentine's Day, Amy was alone in her Manhattan apartment. She couldn't help thinking about her failed marriage and how lonely she now was, and she became more and more miserable. Her doorbell sounded, and when she answered, it was David, a work colleague. David was only five foot three inches in height, rather plump, balding, and wore thick-lensed spectacles. In his arms he held a massive bouquet of red roses. Amy's face lit up when she saw him standing there with the roses, and she was just about to thank him for the Valentine gesture when he said, "I found these down here at your door."

"Really?" Amy said, and she examined the roses, but there was no little note – no indication as to who had sent them. She looked up and down the corridor, baffled.

"Another admirer, obviously," said David, as he walked into the apartment. Amy was intrigued by the roses, and she sat drinking wine that evening, speculating on the identity of her admirer. She suspected and hoped that it was the man who worked as a bartender at a wine bar she often visited after work with her friends. His name was Matt. Throughout the evening Amy talked about Matt, and about his sense of humour, and how wide his shoulders were, and the cute way he smiled lop-sidedly. At one point in her ramblings, Amy said to David, "Hey, *you* didn't leave those roses at my door did you …?"

"No, I did not," said David, avoiding eye contact with her. "I'd never do anything as cheesy as that."

Amy jokingly replied, "… because if you did, David, you'd be wasting your time. You're the best friend a person could have, but you know the type of man I go for."

"Yes … I know … I'm not anyone's type of guy," sighed David resignedly. After a pensive few moments he added, "I wish people could see the inside of a person, instead of just the thin outer layer," and in a barely audible voice David added, "there's so much love in my soul."

Embarrassed at having revealed his true feelings, he made some excuse and left.

On the following day, Amy walked into the wine bar after work, and made a remark to Matt about some anonymous admirer leaving her a bouquet of roses. Matt smiled, exuding his usual charm. After a few glasses of wine, Amy asked the attractive bartender if he had left the flowers. She had to know.

"Maybe," said Matt.

That night, Matt went back to Amy's apartment and stayed the night. It was the beginning of an intense and passionate affair, which lasted until August – when Amy discovered that he was married with two lovely young daughters. She found out in the worst possible way; she was walking hand in hand with Matt one morning down Fifth Avenue, when they bumped into the children's mother. Matt's wife gave him a choice there and then – Amy or her. Matt chose his wife, and left Amy standing on the spot, crushed and humiliated. The end of the affair had a devastating effect on her and now, after work, she avoided going out and became a virtual recluse.

One unbearable Tuesday morning, a few weeks after being ditched by Matt, Amy decided to call her workplace and say she was sick. She left a message on her boss's answering machine. She swallowed a sleeping pill, and curled up in bed, feeling sorry for herself. She wished that David was there to share her troubles, but he had started a new job in Manhattan.

Suddenly, at around a quarter to nine, Amy saw David's kind, bespectacled face looking at her as she drifted into a dream. He was smiling affectionately at her, and suddenly, in the dream, she fell in love with him. She realised what he had said about people never looking at the beauty and love within a person, just the skin-deep shallow beauty.

Amy woke up with her heart pounding, and felt as if she was in love for the first time in her life. She went to call David, but noticed that she had a text message on her cell phone. She felt dizzy as she read it. It said, 'Amy, I love you, and always will love you. *I* left the roses at your door. I can tell you now, because it doesn't matter anymore. Love, David.'

Still holding the phone and wondering what the last line of the message meant, Amy groggily sat down and switched on the television. On the screen, on the CNN channel, were the shocking images of the World Trade Center. The Twin Towers were both engulfed in flames and billowing vast clouds of thick, black smoke. With horror, Amy remembered that David had just started his new job at the World Trade Center. She frantically tried to call him – but the automated voice on the line stated that his cell phone could not be reached.

Amy later discovered that David had died in the terrorist attacks on the Twin Towers. He had been on the one hundred and seventh floor of one of the towers. Like many other victims who knew they were about to die, he had sent a text message to the person he loved. Many heartbreaking telephone calls were made from the towers that morning. David had probably been afraid of rejection, because he imagined he was unattractive, but felt he had nothing to lose by declaring his love for Amy in the last minutes of his life.

On Valentine's Day 2002, Amy said she received a mysterious text message which read, 'Love never dies', and it could not be traced. She says she knows in her heart that it was from David.

I SEE A DARK STRANGER

Madame Rosalind De Vere was a fortune-teller who was also known by many other names in the Liverpool of the forties, fifties and sixties. She had once called herself Madame Zodia during one 'incarnation'.

One lunchtime, in Liverpool, in the summer of 1966, nineteen-year-old Nancy Fenn left Blacklers, the store where she worked, and instead of going to the kiosk to get some cigarettes and a packet of crisps as she usually did, she went with Violet, her sixteen-year-old friend, to the parlour of one Madame De Vere, which was then situated in the Bold Street area. Nancy had heard a lot about the old fortune-teller's amazing predictions, which included the foretelling of her older sister's pregnancy – she had even forecast that she would have twins.

Nancy and Violet climbed the stairs until they reached the dark room over the shop. Nancy sat at a small round table draped with a purple cloth, and facing her sat Madame De Vere, staring directly into her shy blue eyes. The self-conscious girl's eyelashes fluttered. She took half a crown from her purse and gave it to the old woman, and soon the prediction was delivered. No palms were read, no crystal ball was consulted. "I see a dark stranger," said Madame De Vere.

Violet giggled in the darkness somewhere in background.

"Shut up," said Nancy under her breath.

The fortune-teller continued: "He is very tall and very handsome, but beware, my dear, beware! He will come into your life on a Thursday, the last day of this month."

"Why did you say 'beware'? Can you tell me any more?"

"There's a shadow over him, and that usually portends evil, or vice. I can't penetrate that shadow, because it's so dark."

Violet giggled again, and the fortune-teller ordered the girls to leave. The smile was wiped from Violet's face when Madame De Vere called after her, "You won't have much to smile about next week."

Young Violet was terrified by the remark. When she got home her mum was holding a letter.

"Violet, this is from the hospital. They've set a date next week for you to have your tonsils out."

Violet felt faint, and said, "No, I'm fine, Mam. I don't think I need it anymore."

But her mother insisted that she couldn't mess the hospital about. She had suffered recurrent bouts of tonsillitis for years and had waited over eighteen months for the operation.

Fortunately, the tonsillectomy was a success, but shortly after the operation Violet had awakened in pain to find nurses with what appeared to be toothbrushes, frantically rubbing away huge, solid clots in her throat that had formed from unexpected haemorrhaging.

Nancy, meanwhile, waited for the last day of June, which was a Thursday. And on that date, a tall, dark-haired man of about thirty walked into Blacklers. He spoke with a slight Cockney accent, and after Nancy had served him at the till, he remarked on her good looks. The man seemed charming, and he really did have a genuine twinkle in his eye when he looked at Nancy, who had felt herself blush as red as a beetroot. He was holding up a queue of grumbling shoppers, so he walked away, lurked about for a while, then returned to Nancy. His name was Joe Hughes, he said, and he was staying at the YMCA. He was very forward, and asked, "What's your name?" Nancy smiled and gazed shyly at him from under her fringe, as told him it was Nancy.

"Okay, Nancy with the laughing face, I'm going to make a fool of myself now. I'm going to ask you out, because if I don't, I'll regret it for the rest of my life."

Nancy blushed so much that she felt hot all over, especially when she noticed a boy who worked at the store listening to her. That boy, Frankie, also liked Nancy, so to impress him, she decided to accept Joe's romantic offer.

Joe Hughes kissed Nancy's knuckle, and told her to meet him at the YMCA at 7.30pm that night. Then he left. Frankie was gutted, and told Nancy that the man looked far too old for her. Nancy ignored him and said dreamily that Joe's eyes were lovely.

That night, Nancy went to the YMCA on Mount Pleasant and found Joe waiting for her, dressed in the height of fashion. He took her to the Beehive, then on to a nearby club – probably the Mardi Gras. Throughout the evening he behaved like a true gentleman, and paid for a taxi to take her to her Everton home, which really impressed her parents. Two weeks later, in Joe's basement flat on Catherine Street, he and Nancy were sitting intimately together on a sofa when Nancy asked, "What do you think the most attractive part of me is? I mean face-wise? Is it my eyes? People seem to think so."

Joe nodded, and then said a strange thing, "And your neck!" And he put his hand around her neck and smiled. Something in that smile, and in the way he had grasped her neck, made her feel uncomfortable, and she pushed his hand away.

On the following day, Nancy dragged Joe to Bold Street, to visit the fortune-teller once more. She was eager to know if she would be married, have children, and so on. Joe thought it was a complete waste of time, and said so, but went along with her anyway. The couple sat before Madame De Vere, who seemed to be studying Joe intently. She read the couple's future, and then said, "Nancy, I see you wearing his ..." and the fortune-teller seemed to lose her voice.

"You see me wearing his what?" asked Nancy. "His ring?"

Madame De Vere gasped and said: "I see you wearing his ... tie ... it's tight around your neck ... tight ... choking you ... choking you!"

Nancy shook her head and turned to Joe, expecting him to be treating the whole thing as a joke. The look of pure evil on his face chilled her to the bone. In a rage, he stood up and pointed a finger in the fortune-teller's face, "I'll come back for you!" then swung round and left. Nancy rose to follow him, but the old woman held her back saying, "No, don't go after him, he's a murderer."

The fortune-teller led Nancy into the safety of the room next door and locked it. She told the girl that in her vision she had seen her boyfriend strangling women, and dumping those women in a river.

Love is very blind, and despite the fortune-teller's dire warning, Nancy later called at the Catherine Street flat to see her beloved Joe, but he was gone, along with all his belongings.

At that time, there was a serial killer at large in London nicknamed Jack the Stripper, who dumped the naked bodies of his victims in the River Thames. Some had been strangled with a tie, and even their own undergarments. Some thought the killer was the boxer, Freddie Mills, others claimed he was a policeman, but he was never caught. There were also many rumours that the killer had fled the capital and gone north.

Was Nancy's handsome boyfriend the London serial-killer? And had she been saved from his clutches by the old fortune-teller?

THE TELEPATH

In the 1990s, Donna, a twenty-nine-year-old Liverpool woman, was lying in bed one night, about to fall asleep, when she heard familiar voices. They were those of Mike and Liz, the couple next door, but their voices seemed amplified and unnaturally clear. Donna sat up in bed and listened. She quickly discovered that she was not actually hearing the couple next door at all – she was tuning into their very thoughts! She telepathically heard Liz ask her husband if he'd like a coffee, and then Donna read his mind, and distinctly heard him say, "Yes, please". She then picked up a curious inner thought dialogue. Mike pondered to himself: "I wonder if Liz knows about Michelle and me?"

Donna then perceived the mental image Mike had in his mind of Michelle lying naked on a bed and instantly recognised Michelle, a twenty-two-year-old woman who lived across the street.

Donna went downstairs, feeling very uneasy about the strange telepathic ability she had suddenly developed. She wondered if someone had spiked her drink at the pub earlier in the evening. As she made herself a coffee in her kitchen, she sensed that someone was outside, and that the person was feeling desperate. When she peeked through the blinds, she saw a youth in a tracksuit scurrying past. Donna knew at once that the young man was a heroin addict, about to steal to get his next fix. The telepathic state of mind then faded away as mysteriously as it had arrived, and Donna went to bed, wondering if her experience had merely been caused by an over-tired brain.

However, on the following morning, Donna boarded a bus to take her to her office job in the city centre, and during the journey, as the vehicle travelled down Leece Street, the telepathic faculty suddenly returned. Glancing at a schoolgirl, Donna inadvertently read her mind, and felt intense turmoil and anguish because the boy whom the girl had a crush on, was in love with her best friend. Donna next turned her attention to the back of the old woman's head in front of her, and immediately probed the pensioner's nostalgic reminiscences about the Leece Street of many decades ago. Donna beheld misty images of trams passing St Luke's Church.

A man suddenly boarded the bus and sat down next to Donna. She instantly saw an horrific sight, in her mind's eye, of a murder being committed. A woman was being killed in cold blood. The man sitting next to

Donna was a murderer! Donna was almost sick as she read his murderous thoughts. "Get away from me," she yelled, then ran to the front of the bus.

She got off the vehicle in Renshaw Street – and so did the murderer! He chased her into a shop, where Donna pleaded for an assistant to call the police because of what she had seen in her visions – she didn't know what else to call them. Taking her pleas to be the ramblings of a lunatic, the shop assistant escorted her out of the store. She sensed that the killer was lurking nearby, and knew that he was desperate to silence her because she obviously knew about his evil deed.

Donna hailed a cab, jumped into it, and had just directed the driver to take her to work, when the killer rushed to the taxi and yanked open the door. Donna screamed, but the cabby dismissed it as just another domestic incident between a couple. The steely-eyed murderer lunged towards Donna, when a huge man suddenly grabbed him from behind by the collar of his coat. It was Andy, Donna's friend who worked nearby. He had seen the stranger pursuing her to the cab, and didn't like the look of him.

The killer shoved Andy to the ground and sped off. Donna burst into tears, and Andy got in the taxi and told the driver to take them to his house. During the journey, Donna accidentally read Andy's mind and discovered a shocking secret. He had once raped a woman, many years ago, and had served a prison sentence as a result. Donna felt sick. She ordered the cabby to stop, then walked home, without giving Andy any explanation. When she finally got home, she broke down and cried. She thought she was going mad.

Not long afterwards, she saw a photograph of the man who had chased her in the *Liverpool Echo* – he had been arrested for the murder of his wife. She felt huge relief – at least now she knew she wasn't going mad.

Nevertheless, Donna sought psychiatric treatment because she found her telepathic abilities unwanted and disturbing, and gradually, the eerie mind-reading capability faded away.

THE ANSWER MAN

At the base of St John's Beacon in Liverpool city centre, lies the barely recognisable vestiges of Houghton Street. In Edwardian times, there existed a quaint and enchanting tea and coffee shop at Number 8 Houghton Street, called the Japanese Tea Rooms. The place was a welcoming refuge where shoppers with tired feet could recuperate as they sipped refreshing teas such as Sencha, Camomile, Earl Grey and Maccha. The shop's name was something of a misnomer though, because it was also a place in which to indulge in the uplifting caffeine of the richest and most aromatic Mexican and Brazilian coffees.

However, the main attraction of the shop was not the leaves and beans, but the enigmatic old man who owned the premises – Zacharia Walton, also known as the 'Answer Man' because of his incredible wisdom and alleged gift of clairvoyance. A small card, faded with the sun, was displayed in the window of his shop and read:

> *You are in love with someone*
> *But that person doesn't love you?*
> *You have a dream but it won't come true?*
> *You have a problem but there's no solution?*
> *Enquire within at Zacharia's Consulting Booth.*

The booth was accessed via a narrow door in a partition wall at the far end of the shop's interior. The scent of chrysanthemum incense hung in the shadowy, claustrophobic enclosure of the booth, which bore a strong resemblance to a Catholic confessional. There was no illumination in the five-foot by seven-foot room. A curtain which parted in the adjoining room to initiate the consultation period, admitted feeble gaslight through a fine gauze grille. The face of Zacharia Walton would not be visible throughout the sitting. Only his voice would be heard after the client addressed him with his or her problem.

One mellow October afternoon in 1907, thirty-five-year-old Anne Cottrell entered the Japanese Tea Rooms. She whispered to a waitress about the possibility of entering the booth, and was told that Mr Walton would not be available until 3.30pm, which was almost an hour away. Mrs Cottrell therefore left the premises and went window-shopping to kill time. She returned to the tea rooms at 3.25pm and paid the waitress the fee of one shilling. At half-past three the same waitress ushered Mrs Cottrell past the few customers in the room to the booth, where the lady was guided to the old straight-backed chair. She sat facing the grille as the door was closed, throwing the interior of the booth into pitch-blackness. There was a faint thud and a stir of movement next door, followed by the swish of a curtain. Faint bluish light filtered through the grille high above, on the wall facing Mrs Cottrell.

"What is your name?" asked Zacharia, his voice drifting into the claustrophobic cubicle.

"Anne Cottrell," replied the anxious lady, wringing her hands.

"What can I do for you?"

"I think I am being haunted by a ghost," came the reply. There was a lengthy pause. "Hello! Is anybody there?" Mrs Cottrell was quite unnerved by the eerie hiatus.

"Mrs Cottrell, do you work with scissors and cloth?" Zacharia asked.

"Yes, I am a ladies' tailor."

"You have just lost your husband," the elderly seer stated confidently.

"Yes, that is right."

Mrs Cottrell was very impressed and was curious to know what he would say next.

"You *are* being haunted, madam, but not by a ghost," said Zacharia slowly.

"I don't understand," Mrs Cottrell confessed, and she leaned a little nearer to the small aperture in the wall to hear the medium better.

"Your husband is here now," Zacharia informed his client.

Mrs Cottrell was too stunned to answer.

Zacharia muttered something inaudible to someone, then said: "Your husband loved you so much, and he always will, and he tells me that two people are conspiring against you. Please wait one moment. He is divulging more information." Tense seconds elapsed, then Zacharia said, "Go outside and we will talk more."

The old man took the bewildered woman to a quiet corner of the shop and told her that a couple from Anfield were trying to get her committed to an asylum for the insane. Zacharia couldn't provide the first names of the despicable pair, but he felt their surnames had been Dovitt, or Dovey. The man and woman were related to Mrs Cottrell's late husband.

Zacharia said he rarely got involved in the personal business of a client outside the booth, but he was making an exception in this case because he feared for Mrs Cottrell's safety. He frightened her by urging her to get in touch with the police, because the people who were scheming to remove her from society would stop at nothing – even murder. Mrs Cottrell trembled, and the old psychic quickly told the waitress to bring her a strong cup of coffee. As his distressed client cupped her hands around the hot coffee, Zacharia extracted another remarkable piece of information from the ether.

"Mrs Cottrell, do you know of a Mr Valentine?" he queried.

The tailoress blushed and lowered her gaze, "Yes, sir, I do."

A gentle smile broke out on the old man's face. "He's an admirer, I believe." Mrs Cottrell nodded. "He is a good man, and he will see you through all of this. You will marry him."

"Oh," gasped Mrs Cottrell, who was pleasantly shocked by the supernatural disclosure, even in the midst of the other unsettling revelations.

"I'm afraid that is all, Mrs Cottrell."

Old Zacharia suddenly seemed overtaxed by the paranormal experiences, and with a weary expression, he smiled, squeezed Mrs Cottrell's hand, then rose to his feet and left the table for a room at the rear of the shop.

That evening, Anne Cottrell told her close friend Ellen Latham about Zacharia Walton's frightening claims. Mrs Latham reassured her by saying that the old man was a reputable medium who had helped many acquaintances of hers over the years. Later that same evening, Mr Stephen Valentine, a friend of the late Mr Cottrell, called at the house. Mr Valentine knew of Mr Cottrell's relative, George Dovey, who lived in Anfield, but wondered why the man would be conspiring to have Anne committed to an asylum, or even murdered. Mrs Latham was much more perceptive. She knew that Anne Cottrell had once suffered a nervous breakdown several years ago, brought on by the tragic death of her sister in a house fire. It took many years for Anne to regain her mental stability, but thanks to the help of her husband and friends, she pulled through it all and rebuilt her life. Suppose somebody stood to gain something of great value if Anne was either dead or confined to a mental hospital?

Shortly after the death of Mr Cottrell, Anne had claimed that she had often seen her husband's ghost standing in the street, gazing up at her window. The ghost would shake its head and walk off into the twilight. Anne had thought the spectre disapproved of her burgeoning relationship with Mr Valentine. What if it hadn't been a ghost at all, but someone who bore a striking facial resemblance to the widow's late husband. Could that impostor be his cousin, Mr Dovey? Mr Valentine vaguely recalled that George Dovey had worn a large beard when he had last met him five years previously, and he also recalled that Dovey had despised his cousin Cottrell because he had been such a success in life. Ellen Latham was excited by the plausibility of her theory, and she accompanied Mr Valentine to the Dovey's house in Anfield on the following evening.

George Dovey was taken by surprise. He had been about to leave the house to haunt the street where Anne Cottrell lived, and he had even been meticulous enough to wear the same fedora and clothing as that worn by his dead cousin. Dovey's beard had been shaved off, and he looked like a living replica of the late Mr Cottrell. The ghost impersonator was quite speechless, but subsequently denied that he had been attempting to drive Anne Cottrell to insanity so that he could inherit her husband's fortune and property.

Within days, George Dovey and his wife, who was probably a cohort in the contemptible money-making scheme, vacated the house in Anfield and were heard of no more.

The sham apparition of the departed Mr Cottrell immediately ceased haunting the widow Anne. In the summer of 1908, Anne married Stephen Valentine, fulfilling Zacharia's prediction.

OTHER TITLES
Published by The Bluecoat Press

HAUNTED LIVERPOOL 1	Tom Slemen	£5.99
HAUNTED LIVERPOOL 2	Tom Slemen	£5.99
HAUNTED LIVERPOOL 3	Tom Slemen	£5.99
HAUNTED LIVERPOOL 4	Tom Slemen	£5.99
HAUNTED LIVERPOOL 5	Tom Slemen	£5.99
HAUNTED LIVERPOOL 6	Tom Slemen	£5.99
HAUNTED LIVERPOOL 7	Tom Slemen	£5.99
HAUNTED LIVERPOOL 8	Tom Slemen	£5.99
HAUNTED WIRRAL	Tom Slemen	£5.99
WICKED LIVERPOOL	Tom Slemen	£5.99
MYSTERIES	Tom Slemen	£5.99
TOM SLEMEN'S MYSTERIOUS WORLD		£5.99
HAUNTED LIVERPOOL double cassette audio book, read by Tom Slemen		£8.99
A DIFFERENT SKY, UFO'S IN MERSEYSIDE	Tony Eccles	£5.99

Available from all good bookshops
For a free stocklist contact
The Bluecoat Press, 45 Bluecoat Chambers, School Lane, Liverpool L1 3BX
Telephone 0151 707 2390

If you have had a paranormal encounter,
or a supernatural experience of any sort, please drop a line to:

Thomas Slemen
c/o The Bluecoat Press
45 Bluecoat Chambers
School Lane
Liverpool L1 3BX

All correspondence will be answered.